T0301559

ASIAN FINANCIAL STATEMENT ANALYSIS

Detecting Financial Irregularities

CFA Institute is a global community of investment professionals dedicated to driving industry-wide adoption of the highest ethical and analytical standards. Through our programs, conferences, credentialing, and publications, CFA Institute leads industry thinking, helping members of the investment community deepen their expertise. We believe that fair and effective financial markets led by competent and ethically-centered professionals stimulate economic growth. Together—with our 112,000 members from around the world, including 100,000 CFA charterholders—we are shaping an investment industry that serves the greater good.

www.cfainstitute.org

ASIAN FINANCIAL STATEMENT ANALYSIS

Detecting Financial Irregularities

ChinHwee Tan, CFA, CPA
Thomas R. Robinson, CFA, CPA

WILEY

Cover image: (top) © iStockphoto.com / loveguli (bottom) © iStockphoto.com / IS_ImageSource
Cover design: Wiley

Copyright © 2014 by CFA Institute. All rights reserved.

Published by John Wiley & Sons, Inc., Hoboken, New Jersey.
Published simultaneously in Canada.

No part of this publication may be reproduced, stored in a retrieval system, or transmitted in any form
or by any means, electronic, mechanical, photocopying, recording, scanning, or otherwise, except as
permitted under Section 107 or 108 of the 1976 United States Copyright Act, without either the prior
written permission of the Publisher, or authorization through payment of the appropriate per-copy fee to
the Copyright Clearance Center, Inc., 222 Rosewood Drive, Danvers, MA 01923, (978) 750-8400, fax
(978) 646-8600, or on the Web at www.copyright.com. Requests to the Publisher for permission should
be addressed to the Permissions Department, John Wiley & Sons, Inc., 111 River Street, Hoboken, NJ
07030, (201) 748-6011, fax (201) 748-6008, or online at www.wiley.com/go/permissions.

Limit of Liability/Disclaimer of Warranty: While the publisher and author have used their best efforts
in preparing this book, they make no representations or warranties with respect to the accuracy
or completeness of the contents of this book and specifically disclaim any implied warranties of
merchantability or fitness for a particular purpose. No warranty may be created or extended by sales
representatives or written sales materials. The advice and strategies contained herein may not be suitable
for your situation. You should consult with a professional where appropriate. Neither the publisher nor
author shall be liable for any loss of profit or any other commercial damages, including but not limited
to special, incidental, consequential, or other damages.

For general information on our other products and services or for technical support, please contact our
Customer Care Department within the United States at (800) 762-2974, outside the United States at
(317) 572-3993, or fax (317) 572-4002.

Wiley publishes in a variety of print and electronic formats and by print-on-demand. Some material
included with standard print versions of this book may not be included in e-books or in print-on-
demand. If this book refers to media such as a CD or DVD that is not included in the version you
purchased, you may download this material at http://booksupport.wiley.com. For more information
about Wiley products, visit www.wiley.com.

ISBN 978-1-118-48652-8 (Hardcover)
ISBN 978-1-118-54259-0 (ePDF)
ISBN 978-1-118-48665-8 (ePub)

Printed in the United States of America.
10 9 8 7 6 5 4 3 2 1

ChinHwee Tan

To my wife and fellow Chartered Accountant, Michelle Lee—for your constant urging during our university days to study accounting harder, without which this book would never have been written. Thank you for being a good wife and mother to our three lovely children, Brian, Kylie, and Sarah; may they learn the importance of integrity and the dangers of cutting corners from this book.

To my parents, for exposing their children to education in the broadest sense. Your holistic parenting in spite of our financial limitations imbued us with the confidence and abilities to pursue our dreams, be they in the arts or finance.

To my business partner, Girish Kumar, and my colleagues at Apollo Global Management, for their support, and more importantly, our friendship.

Finally, to the many humbling experiences throughout my career, including my first credit default during the Asian Financial Crisis in 1998. Thank you for the perceptiveness and appreciation that learning is a lifelong endeavor.

Thomas R. Robinson

To my wife, Linda, and my late father, Clarence E. Robinson.

To the accounting faculty at Case Western Reserve University that shaped my early thinking on accounting and the importance of high ethical conduct, including but not limited to Gary Previts, Rob Kauer, Tom Sturgis, and Larry Phillips.

To my former colleagues at Deloitte and University of Miami who helped further refine and shape my thinking on the topics in this book, particularly Paul Munter, Kay Tatum, Oscar Holzmann, and Elaine Henry.

Last but not least, to the authors of books required in the CFA curriculum that demonstrated how to practically apply accounting knowledge in evaluating financial statements, including Gerald White, Tony Sohndi, and Howard Schilit.

CONTENTS

CHAPTER 3
Detecting Overstated Financial Position   47

CHAPTER 4
Detecting Earnings Management   73

CHAPTER 5
Detecting Overstated Operating Cash Flows   107

FOREWORD

Asian Financial Statement Analysis is an important work and a welcome addition to the discipline of forensic accounting and detection of accounting anomalies in financial reports. Tan and Robinson's major contribution is to show, through recent actual vignettes, how the tricks are played out in Asian companies. Unlike many companies based in the West with a longer tradition (and rules) concerning strong corporate governance, Tan and Robinson show that investors must be even more vigilant in performing due diligence on Asian companies that unfortunately often engage in non-arm's-length transactions.

The book is written clearly for a non-technical audience, providing (1) user-friendly checklists to be adopted by any securities analyst; (2) lessons to be learned by studying the frauds at Satyam, Sino-Forest, and Olympus, among others; and (3) reviews at the end of each chapter that highlight key lessons learned.

Analysts, auditors, and other stakeholders also benefit by learning lessons from colossal financial reporting failures at companies. Tan and Robinson have provided readers a great service by studying debacles at the often less-studied Asian companies and writing this book, which shares the lessons from such debacles.

Dr. Howard M. Schilit
CEO of Schilit Forensics, LLC
Author of *Financial Shenanigans: How to Detect Accounting Gimmicks & Fraud in Financial Reports*

GENESIS OF THIS BOOK

The idea for this book first came from the chairman of one of the largest and most iconic stock exchanges in the world. She appealed to my strong passion to uplift the Asian corporate governance standard and urged me to write a book on forensic accounting.

My first humbling reminder of why I need to develop a systematic way to intelligently read quantitative (and qualitative) data in the investments I made came when I experienced my first credit default during the Asian crisis in 1998. My skill-set further improved when I worked for U.S. authorities on a number of fraud cases in 2001 to 2002, the "go-go" era when WorldCom and Enron dominated head-lines. Since then, I have been given the privilege of doing pro-bono advisory work on forensic accounting cases for regulators in a number of countries.

With the book idea in mind, I immediately approached former accounting professor Tom Robinson to collaborate on the manuscript. As a Managing Director at the CFA Institute, Tom is a natural partner. He has done seminars on account-ing fraud with me, and his knowledge base in this topic is extensive. Tom readily agreed, as both of us are determined to do our small part in improving corporate governance standards and analysis in Asia. We hope readers will be able to benefit from both theoretical and practical application of accounting principles.

ChinHwee Tan, CFA, CPA

ACKNOWLEDGMENTS

We would like to acknowledge the assistance and guidance of quite a few individuals who provided commentary on early drafts of this manuscript and performed research on the cases used in this book: Emilie Herman, our editor at Wiley; Jerome Tan; Paul Bernard, Goldman Sachs (retired); and Rob Gowen, Michael McMillan, Jason Voss, Jerry Pinto, Greg Siegel, and David Larrabee at CFA Institute.

INTRODUCTION

It was like riding a tiger, not knowing how to get off without being eaten.

Ramalinga Raju, founder and former chairman of Satyam

Satyam, founded in 1987, was one of the largest information technology (IT) consultancies in the world. Then a stock darling of India, the company boasted of board members from the "who's who" of the Indian community; nevertheless, its fall from grace was swift and terminal with this letter:

Dear Board Members, it is with deep regret and tremendous burden that I am carrying on my conscience that I would like to bring the following facts to your notice. . . .

So began Ramalinga Raju, founder and former chairman of Satyam, in his resignation letter as he confessed to cooking the books in January 2008, admitting that real profit and cash positions of Satyam were over 90 percent lower than the figures in the accounts. Satyam's share price collapsed about 90 percent within days. There is an idiom in Chinese, Qi Hu Nan Xia (骑虎难下) telling of the difficulties of dismounting a tiger—clearly, the tiger got the better of Raju.

Today, Satyam operates as a subsidiary of Tech Mahindra Limited after its takeover, subsequent to the unraveling of its fraudulent accounts, by the Mahindra Group in 2009. The company's consolidated 2013 revenues exceed US$2.7 billion, making it one of India's five largest IT services companies. The combined firm today employs 84,000 employees serving 540 clients across 46 nations. Current management holds fast that they have put the past behind them and asserts that "by 2015 [Satyam] will be a US$5bn company."

In their classic book, *Security Analysis*, now in its sixth edition, Benjamin Graham and David Dodd highlighted the importance of a careful and fundamental evaluation of a company's business and financial statements. Based on this book and his other works, Benjamin Graham became known as the "father of value

1

investing."[1] Value investing focuses on buying good companies at good prices—starting with the question of whether an investment is cheap and then why is it cheap. If it is cheap because the market has overlooked an important aspect of the future prospects for the company, then it may indeed be good value. Some stocks, however, are cheap because they deserve to be, and the market may properly recognize that the future business and cash flow prospects are poor. However, some stocks are richly priced by the market when in fact these are merely the result of management inflating earnings, cash flow, or the financial position of the firm.

In hindsight, it turned out that Satyam belonged to the latter category. Its story was simply too good to be true: bogus customer receipts and fictitious cash balances were created to balance the double-entry accounting books so as to conceal the overstatement of profits, similar to Parmalat, the Italian dairy and food corporation, whose collapse in 2003 resulted in one of the largest fraud cases in Europe's history.

So how does one detect accounting games such as those played by Satyam and Parmalat?

Fingerprints were first used in 1905 as a forensic tool in the trial of a South East London murder case. It was the maiden use of forensic science to establish guilt or innocence. The double-entry accounting system, which traces its roots back to the fifteenth century when Luca Pacioli first penned his encyclopedia of mathematics, has been called "one of the greatest advances in the history of business and commerce."[2] More important, it is to investment professionals what fingerprints are to crime scene investigators and has been aptly identified as the building block of forensic accounting. This system, which underlies even the most sophisticated accounting systems today, creates a framework of checks and balances that enable the discerning analyst to detect fraudulent accounting.

This book is written to provide a practical guide to performing forensic financial analyses of the financial statements of Asian companies. It is written with the global investor in mind, and we hope it will help you to avoid investing in companies that are not in as strong a financial condition as their reported financial statements may appear or to identify companies that may be overpriced relative to their true profitability (presenting a potential short sale opportunity). With this book, we hope to share our experiences in financial statement analysis globally and Asia specifically. The disparity of business practices, both intraregionally and intranationally, is a hallmark of Asia; we hope this book will be the start of your journey to navigating the intricacies of investing in Asian businesses.

WHY FOCUS ON SCANDALS IN ASIA?

As previously noted, accounting scandals, such as Parmalat in Europe and Satyam in India, can occur globally. Much has been documented about the international nature

EXHIBIT I.1   Chinese Stock Market Returns Have Lagged Behind GDP Growth

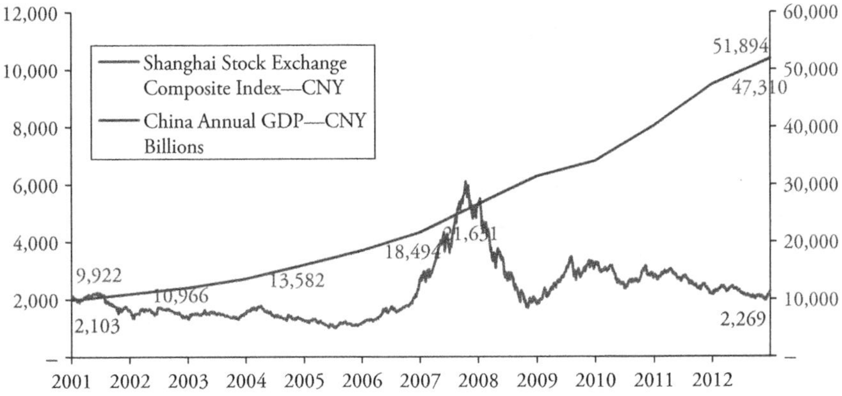

Sources: Bloomberg, National Bureau of Statistics of China.

of these scandals, from Europe's Ivar Kreuger, the "Swedish Match King," to Canada's Bre-X fraud, to the Worldcom case in the United States. However, significantly less has been written about cases in the Asia region, many of which are quite recent.

Furthermore, corporate governance has been the Achilles' heel for minority equity shareholders in Asia. Despite being publicly traded, many companies are still effectively controlled by the founder or his family; there is nothing inherently wrong with this, but the real winners in many companies are not the minority shareholders. For example, in China, despite the strong economic growth that saw its gross domestic product (GDP) more than double over the past decade, the domestic Shanghai Composite index, which represents the largest listed companies in China, has virtually stayed at the same level since 2001 as shown in Exhibit I.1. This is similar to that of Korea from 1990 to 2005, when the KOSPI stayed flat despite a 3.5 times rise in the country's GDP.

Underperformance of key Asian equity indices in spite of resounding economic growth in both countries may be, in part, attributed to the lack of corporate governance in these markets. There is a strong need for forensic accounting in Asia to help tackle this issue, as well as to raise Asia's standards of corporate governance, going beyond accounting manipulation to include board structure, compensation practices, and the like. This will ultimately unlock value for minority equity holders. While some would argue that stock market returns are not a suitable proxy for GDP growth, the fact is that many companies (and their founders) were big winners in the GDP acceleration and became very rich overnight—something that failed to trickle down to minority shareholders.

HOW THIS BOOK IS ORGANIZED

This book begins by presenting a framework that enables those analyzing financial statements to detect irregularities where the company may be overstating their profits, financial position, or cash flow. Subsequent chapters drill down to show detailed evaluation techniques and warning signs for the most common games that companies play. In each of these chapters, we provide practical applications using real Asia-based companies throughout the chapter. Each chapter also presents a checklist of analysis techniques and warning signs to look for. At the end of each chapter, we present full case studies of real Asia-based companies to demonstrate the techniques in a holistic manner.

Chapter 1, "A Framework for Evaluating Financial Irregularities," provides the key to the book. In this chapter, we present the basics of the accounting system, which creates the checks and balances essential to creating financial statements and detecting irregularities within them. Some of you may have studied accounting in college and may (but more likely not) recall the dreaded "debits" and "credits." Fear not—this is not your typical accounting text, and we will not muddy the waters with such minutiae. Instead, we demonstrate how the primary financial statements fit together and how this information can be used to detect problems and highlight where more questions are warranted. In this and subsequent chapters, we provide real-life examples of accounting games that companies play in Asia. It is important to note, however, that the framework and techniques we present are equally applicable to companies globally. In fact, the techniques were developed by the authors' study and experience with companies operating worldwide, not just in Asia.

Chapter 2, "Detecting Overstated Earnings," examines one of the most common goals of unscrupulous managers: overstating profits relative to the underlying reality. We address cases that range from aggressive reporting (premature revenue recognition) to outright fraud (reporting nonexistent revenues). In this chapter, and in Chapters 3 through 7, we detail cases of companies that have been accused, but not necessarily ascertained guilty, of manipulating their reported results. Do note that these cases may overlap with material in other chapters due to the often plural nature of accounting manipulation.

Chapter 3, "Detecting Overstated Financial Position," takes a look at companies that attempt to make their financial position look stronger than it really is. While commonly associated with the overstatement of assets, that is not always the case. The company may want to understate both assets and liabilities, which improves profitability ratios (such as return on assets) or debt ratios (by making them look smaller).

Chapter 4, "Detecting Earnings Management," takes the material in Chapter 3 one step further, addressing multiyear manipulation. In a bid to smooth the volatility of earnings or manage the perceived trajectory of earnings, a company may purposefully understate earnings in the current year with the expectation of using this "cookie jar" reserve to boost earnings in later years.

Chapter 5, "Detecting Overstated Operating Cash Flows," examines how companies may massage reported numbers to inflate some measure of cash flow such as operating cash flow. Often, but not always, this accompanies an overstatement of earnings, as presented in Chapter 3.

Chapter 6, "Evaluating Corporate Governance and Related-Party Issues," examines the impact of weak corporate governance on reported results. Weak corporate governance provides opportunities for the activities presented in Chapters 3 through 5 by permitting managers or majority shareholders to engage in related-party transactions to enrich themselves at the expense of other shareholders.

Chapter 7, "Summary and Guidance," pulls it all together and summarizes things to look out for when evaluating the financial statements of Asian companies—the so-called red flags of corporate accounting.

AS YOU BEGIN

This book is designed to teach you practical techniques that you can keep in the back of your mind as you review financial statements for potential investment, whether you suspect irregularities or not. It is also designed as a more permanent reference to use when you suspect problems at a company. Read the chapters thoroughly now—particularly Chapter 1—and use the checklists at the end to help guide you in the future.

NOTES

1. Benjamin Graham is also notable in that he was one of the earliest proponents of a rating system for financial analysts, which became the CFA Program. The first CFA examination was offered in 1963 in North America, and exams are administered globally by the CFA Institute today.
2. Jane Gleeson-Shite, *Double Entry: How the Merchants of Venice Created Modern Finance* (New York: W. W. Norton & Company, 2012), 93.

CHAPTER 1

A FRAMEWORK FOR EVALUATING FINANCIAL IRREGULARITIES

This chapter presents the basics of the accounting system, which creates the checks and balances essential to creating financial statements and detecting irregularities within them. The chapter demonstrates how the primary financial statements fit together and how this information can be used to detect problems and highlight where more questions are warranted. With this framework, you will have the basic tools to spot the warning signs in a company's financials if something is amiss.

This chapter examines the framework of relationships between the main financial statements—known to accountants as the articulation of financial statements—and shows the reader how to evaluate the possibility that a company is engaged in accounting games. Due to these interrelationships, a company that overstates its profits on its income statement cannot do so without also overstating its assets or understating its liabilities on the balance sheet. If a company artificially reduces its liabilities to strengthen its perceived financial condition, it will likely need to reduce its assets as well. Should a company artificially inflate its operating cash flow with no corresponding increase in the actual cash balance, it will need to reduce its investing or financing cash flows.

The most common case of fraudulent activity is an overstatement of profits—the first example above. In these cases, an overstatement of assets usually occurs through accounts receivable from customers, inventory, or some sort of intangible or other unique asset. As a result, a common method of detecting fraudulent activity is to look for unusual increases in asset accounts that have not been adequately explained in the footnotes or by management. This chapter discusses how the interrelatedness of the financial statements may assist in picking up warning signs of accounting manipulation.

ARTICULATION OF FINANCIAL STATEMENTS

The three major financial statements of interest to the analyst[1] are the income statement, the statement of cash flows, and the balance sheet.

The income statement shows the revenues from operating the business, the associated expenses, gains and losses, and the net profit over a period of time. It is a primary source for measuring the profitability of the business.

While profits are nice to have, you cannot pay employees, suppliers, creditors, and others with profits—payment requires cash. Another important statement is therefore the statement of cash flows, which presents the cash receipts, cash payments, and net cash flow of the business (typically separated into three activities—operating, investing, and financing). This statement helps assess how well the company is doing at converting profits into cash flow, investing for the future, and the sources of financing or repayment of capital.

The balance sheet, also known as the statement of financial position or statement of financial condition, shows a snapshot of the assets or resources of the business at a point in time and the claims against those resources by creditors (liabilities) and investors (owners' equity). The balance sheet is also the core financial statement, which connects the other financial statements over time. The balance sheet reflects the so-called accounting equation, which has been with us for many hundreds of years and forces the articulation of financial statements. In the simplest terms, the accounting equation is as portrayed in Exhibit 1.1.

The accounting equation is a given and must always balance—hence the term *balance sheet*. The balance sheet depicts the accounting equation at a given point in time and must balance. If you ever come across a company whose balance sheet does not balance (one of the authors has seen this only twice in his 25-year career), your analysis becomes infinitely easier—discard this company's financial statements and find another company to invest in (or sell this one short!).

EXHIBIT 1.1   The Accounting Equation for Financial Statements

Now let's look at an extended version of the balance sheet in accounting equation format and how the income statement and cash flow statement fit into the balance sheet.

The top panel of Exhibit 1.2 shows the balance sheet at the beginning of the period and the end of the period (usually a year but sometimes quarterly or semiannually) and some of the common types of assets, liabilities, and owners' equity. For example, common assets include cash, accounts receivables (amounts due from customers), inventory (goods held for sale), investments, property (such as land, buildings, and equipment), and other assets such as intangible assets, prepaid items, and deposits. Liabilities can be due in the short term or long term and can be monies owed to suppliers, banks, employees, and other creditors. Owners' equity includes capital contributed by the owners, profits retained in the business not yet distributed to the owners (retained earnings), and some special items such as other comprehensive income (typically, gains and losses not yet reported on the income statement).

The middle panel presents an abbreviated form of the income statement. Note the distinction between revenues and expenses versus gains and losses. Revenues and expenses are reported on a gross basis and related to the main operating activities of the business. For example, if the business is a restaurant, then meals sold to customers are reported as revenues for the full amount received from customers with a separate expense reported on the income statement for the cost of the meal sold (both the revenue and expense are reported gross). However, if that same restaurant has an extra piece of equipment it is no longer using and sells that equipment to a used equipment dealer, then the sales price and remaining undepreciated cost of the equipment are netted to determine whether there is a gain or loss, and this net gain or loss is reported separately in the non-operating portion of the income statement. We will later see how some companies try to inflate revenues (but not profits) by reporting such sales in the operating section of the income statement.

The bottom panel presents an abbreviated cash flow statement. The net cash flows (cash received less cash paid) for operating, investing, and financing activities are each summarized and then totaled to arrive at the overall net cash flow of the company for the period.

The income and cash flow statements are directly tied to the change in the balance sheet over the period as shown in the upper panel. Any increase or decrease in net income from the income statement results in an increase or decrease in retained earnings and hence owners' equity on the balance sheet. Similarly, any increase or decrease in cash from the cash flow statement is directly reflected in the change in the cash level on the balance sheet. In this manner the financial statements are all tied together, and those companies that want to artificially make themselves look better cannot manipulate one financial statement without impacting either another financial statement or an offsetting item on the same financial statement.

EXHIBIT 1.2 Balance Sheet (top), Income Statement (middle), and Cash Flow Statement (bottom)

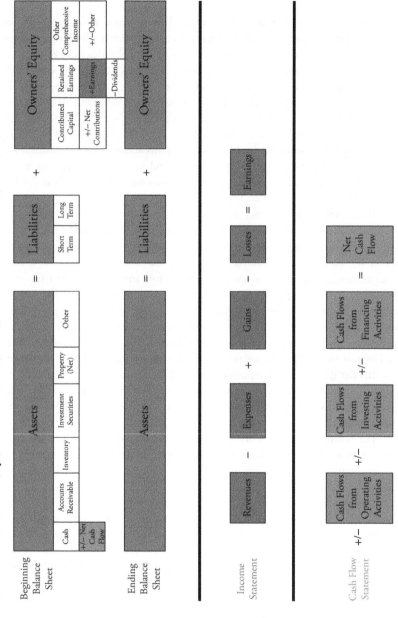

Let's say that a company increases its revenue by making a legitimate cash for services sale to a customer. Revenues and net income increase as depicted in Exhibit 1.3 (to keep it simple we will ignore income tax effects for this example). On the balance sheet shown in Exhibit 1.4, owners' equity increases as a result of net income's increasing, and cash increases as a result of cash collection (this would also be reflected as an operating cash flow on the cash flow statement). A similar result would occur if the sale were made on credit terms. Initially, accounts receivable would increase rather than cash, as the customer has not yet paid. However, when the customer pays, the accounts receivable balance will decline and the cash balance will increase. This should occur in a fairly short window of time depending on the credit terms granted.

However, if a company increases its revenue by making a fictitious sale, no cash is received. They cannot simply increase revenue without recording some adjustment on the balance sheet; otherwise, the balance sheet would not balance. Owners' equity would increase from the increase in net income, while assets and liabilities would remain the same, and the accounting system will not allow this. In order to get the accounting equation and balance sheet to balance, a company recording fictitious revenue must also either overstate assets or understate liabilities. For this type of transaction the most common offset is to overstate assets through an increase in accounts receivable. Because cash is never received, the accounts receivable balance will not go down in the future and in fact will increase rapidly over time—it keeps getting bigger and bigger and bigger. In such frauds there is a limit, and eventually the bubble must burst. Elevated accounts receivable growth relative to revenues can be a sign of inflated revenues.

EXHIBIT 1.3   Increase in Revenue

EXHIBIT 1.4   Balance Sheet Impact

Application: Sino-Forest Corporation

Sino-Forest Corporation came up with a creative way to deal with the increase in accounts receivable resulting from fraudulent timber sales (among other fraudulent activities). Sino-Forest created other companies that it effectively controlled and engaged in fraudulent purchase and sales of timber. In this manner, both accounts receivable and accounts payable (a liability for amounts due to alleged suppliers for timber purchases) would have been overstated. Sino-Forest engaged in an additional scheme to offset the receivables and payables between the controlled "customers" and "suppliers." Of course, the offset was not perfect since the sales prices exceeded the purchase prices. More on Sino-Forest in later chapters!

ACCRUALS AND DEFERRALS

To further our understanding of the interrelationship among the income statement, the cash flow statement, and the balance sheet, let's take a look at the accrual basis of accounting that is used to generate the income statement. The accrual basis (sometimes referred to by students as the "cruel basis") of accounting requires that revenue be recognized on the income statement when earned (rather than when cash is received) and that expenses be recognized when incurred or matched with their associated revenue (rather than when the cash is paid). These differences between the accrual-based income statement and the cash flow statement result in accruals and deferrals that are reflected on the balance sheet. Common accruals and deferrals are summarized in Exhibit 1.5. For example, one that we addressed earlier relates to revenue. If revenue is reported on the income statement before cash is received (the normal situation), then the cash flow occurs after the corresponding revenue is reflected on the income statement. As a result, an asset (accounts receivable) is created. Conversely, let's say that a company is in a business where cash is collected before services are rendered, the classic example being the airline business. You buy your ticket online and pay with your credit card. The airline receives cash from the credit card company right away but has not delivered services to you yet and cannot report the revenue until you fly to your destination. In this case, the cash flow occurs before the revenue is reported on the income statement, and a liability is reported on the balance sheet until services are delivered. This liability is called *unearned revenue* or *deferred revenue*.

Let's take a look at expenses. If a company pays its employees weekly and the year-end occurs between payroll dates, the company must accrue the wages owed

EXHIBIT 1.5   Common Accruals and Deferrals

	Revenue	Expense
Cash Flows Occur Later Than Reflected in Earnings	Asset Accounts Receivable	Liability Accrued Expenses Deferred Tax Liability Contingencies Contra Asset Allowance for Doubtful Accounts
Cash Flows Occur Before Reflected in Earnings	Liability Unearned Revenue Deferred Revenue	Asset Property and Equipment Prepaid Expense Deferred Tax Asset Deferred Expenses

to employees for the partial week and report this as an expense on the income statement even though it has not yet been paid. In this case, the cash flow occurs later than reflected in the income statement for an expense and a liability is created (called *accrued wages* or more simply *accrued expenses*). However, if a company purchases equipment for cash in the current year and that equipment will be used to generate revenue for five years, then the total cost of the equipment is not recorded immediately as an expense. Instead, the cost of that equipment is recognized as an expense over time (termed depreciation), and "matched" to the revenues that it helped to generate. In this case, the cash flow for an expense occurs before it is reflected in the income statement and an asset is created—Plant, Property, and Equipment.

Once again, we see how the income statement, cash flow statement, and balance sheet are intertwined. If an analyst focuses his efforts solely on evaluating the income statement, he or she will overlook telltale signs that appear on the balance sheet and/or cash flow statement. We will use this framework in the remainder of this chapter and subsequent chapters, so you will want to come back to this section until the material is second nature.

TYPICAL ACCOUNTING GAMES

Given the number of transactions a typical company engages in and the complexity of financial statements, there are numerous opportunities for companies to manipulate their financial statements. There are, however, some common themes that are seen when accounting scandals over time are examined. The most common issues can be classified into five categories, as depicted in Exhibit 1.6.

In this chapter, we will briefly introduce each of these themes, which will be explored in depth with real company examples in subsequent chapters.

Overstating Earnings

Both investors and creditors are interested in the level of profits of a company. The higher the earnings or profit, the more can be returned to investors and creditors or invested for the future. Consequently, the most common motivation for accounting games comes from a desire to make earnings look better than they actually are. This can be accomplished by overstating revenues or gains (Exhibit 1.7) or understating expenses or losses (Exhibit 1.8). Some companies go to extremes by doing both.

In any of these cases, the company's earnings and hence retained earnings on the balance sheet will be overstated. In order for the balance sheet to balance, the

EXHIBIT 1.6   Categories for Accounting Scandals

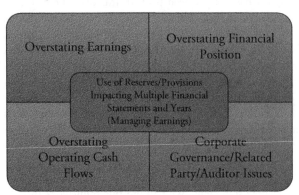

EXHIBIT 1.7   Overstating Revenues or Gains

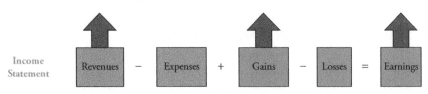

EXHIBIT 1.8   Understating Expenses or Losses

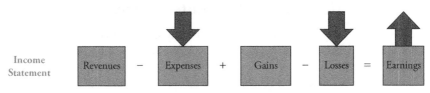

EXHIBIT 1.9   Potential Balance Sheet Impacts

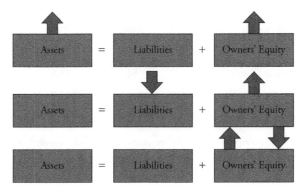

company must do one of the following: overstate assets, understate liabilities, or understate some other equity account (most likely other comprehensive earnings). These possibilities are shown by the arrows in Exhibit 1.9.

The most common result is an overstatement of assets. In the case where revenue is overstated, the most likely asset to be overstated is accounts receivable. In the most extreme case, the company is reporting fictitious revenue for which no cash is ever collected, and the accounts receivable balance grows continuously over time. In other cases, the company may be very aggressive about how it reports revenue and report it before a transaction has taken place or before the revenue is truly earned (e.g., reporting revenue when a contract is signed even though delivery is to occur in the future or the contract relates to the use of the asset over time rather than an immediate sale). In such cases, accounts receivable will increase in the current period at a faster rate than it should but would (hopefully) be collected in a subsequent period. Since fraudulent behavior is repetitive, even in these latter cases, the accounts receivable balance will continue to grow at a faster pace relative to what it should.

Application: Satyam Computer Services Limited

Satyam was a large technology services company in India that was found to have falsified its revenue, income, and level of interest-bearing deposits (an asset) from 2003 to 2008. Let us take a look at some relevant data from its annual financial statements before the scandal was uncovered:

In Millions of US$	FYE March 2008	FYE March 2007	Change
Revenue	2,138.1	1,461.4	+46%
Trade Receivables—Short Term (Asset)	598.8	396.1	+51%
Trade Receivables—Long Term (Asset)	38.2	21.2	+80%
Unbilled Revenue (Asset)*	81.5	38.6	+111%
Investments in Bank Deposits (Asset)**	894.8	782.7	+14%
Total of these asset accounts (in US$mn)	1,613.3	1,238.6	+374.70

*Revenue that has been reported on the income statement as earned—usually from long-term contracts based on the percentage complete.
**Reported as long term in FYE 2007 and short term in FYE 2008.

First, note that revenue was growing at a very rapid pace, which would be a good thing if it was real. The problem is that the three receivables items on the balance sheet were all growing at a pace much greater than revenue. If the company is doing an adequate job of collecting from customers, then receivables growth should not be materially higher than revenue growth. The rapid growth here indicates a problem (perhaps not fraud, but it is a warning sign that more due diligence is necessary). The most unusual item on the balance sheet is an amount that was reported separate from cash—Investments in Bank Deposits. This is quite unusual and is an indicator that perhaps the auditors were provided with different substantiation for these accounts than what they normally see for cash; there certainly must have been a reason why this amount was treated separately. The increase in the receivables accounts plus the investments in bank deposits was US$374.7 million. According to the United States Securities and Exchange Commission lawsuit on this matter, Satyam overstated revenue by US$430.4 million just in FYE March 2008. It turned out that cumulatively over 90 percent of the cash and bank balances reported on the balance sheet (most notably this Investments in Bank Deposits line item) did not exist. You can clearly see how the overstatement of revenue resulted in an overstatement of assets and the warning signs that something was amiss.

EXHIBIT 1.10   Moving Gains "Up" the Income Statement

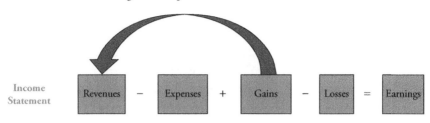

In the case where expenses are understated, there is typically a corresponding overstatement of assets. One example is where a company sells goods (inventory) and reports the revenue on the income statement but fails to transfer the cost of that inventory (which is an asset on the balance sheet) to cost of goods sold (an expense) on the income statement. Earnings are therefore overstated, as are assets (inventory). Over time, this results in a large increase in the inventory balance on the balance sheet.

Another method of understating expenses is to defer their recognition on the income statement. This could be done by misclassifying an expense as a purchase of plant, property, and equipment resulting in an asset on the balance sheet or by creating another type of deferred asset. Some companies have created special categories on their balance sheet for these deferred expenses such as "deferred customer acquisition costs." Sometimes this may be legitimate such as in the insurance industry, but other times it is simply a way to avoid reporting marketing expenses on the income statement.

Many analysts focus on subcomponents of earnings rather than the bottom line—net earnings or net profit. For example, it is common to focus on operating earnings to see how the company is doing from its core business. While it is certainly good to understand how much of a company's profits come from normal recurring operations, we must also understand that companies are aware of this and may try to mislead us. One common ploy of unscrupulous managers is to inappropriately report non-operating gains as part of operating revenues (and to do so on a gross rather than net basis). (See Exhibit 1.10.) This overstates both revenues and operating earnings but has no effect on the bottom-line net earnings.

Another option is to move expenses down the income statement and classify them as a "special" or "extraordinary" loss to make normal operating earnings look larger. (See Exhibit 1.11.)

We will explore examples of overstating earnings in more detail in Chapter 2.

Overstating Financial Position

Overstating financial position is an accounting ploy used to make a company's balance sheet look stronger—usually by understating the liabilities of the company. As

EXHIBIT 1.11   Moving Expenses "Down" the Income Statement

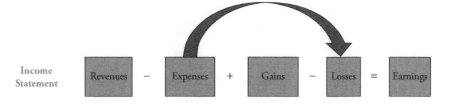

EXHIBIT 1.12   Overstating Financial Position on the Balance Sheet

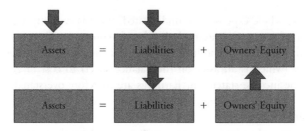

we saw earlier, the company cannot simply remove liabilities from the balance sheet or fail to record them without impacting some other aspect of the balance sheet (and perhaps the income statement and cash flow statement). If liabilities are understated, then either assets must be understated or owners' equity must be overstated, as shown in Exhibit 1.12.

In the first case, where assets or liabilities are understated, the company can take an equal amount of assets and liabilities off of the balance sheet—for example, by transferring them to some type of special-purpose entity or other entity whereby they might be able to avoid consolidating those assets and liabilities with the main company's assets and liabilities. How does this improve the financial position? Are assets not a good thing? Well, yes and no. Let us look at a simple example:

Assets	HKD 10,000,000
Liabilities	HKD 8,000,000
Owners' equity	HKD 2,000,000
Net earnings	HKD 500,000

Common ratios used by analysts are Liabilities to Assets and Return on Assets (Net Earnings / Total Assets). For this company, liabilities to assets are 0.80, or

80 percent, and return on assets is 0.05, or 5 percent. If this company were able to remove HKD 5 million of assets and liabilities from its balance sheet by accounting magic, they would achieve liabilities to assets of 0.60, or 60 percent, and return on assets of 0.10, or 10 percent. They now look less risky (lower level of debt) and more profitable (higher return on assets).

A common example of the second case is for a company to fail to record a liability that would also result in an expense (also overstating earnings). For example, the company may know that it has a liability related to an environmental loss and fail to record either the liability or the loss, overstating earnings and the company's financial position.

Application: Olympus Corporation

Olympus Corporation is a Japan-based manufacturer of precision machinery and instruments founded in 1919. In 2011, it was discovered that Olympus had engaged in a series of complex maneuvers to keep a significant loss, and hence a liability, off of its financial statements since the 1990s, making its financial position look better than it was for many years. It is estimated that the loss was slightly less than ¥100 billion in 1990. For many years Olympus kept the loss off of its own books by transferring financial assets that have declined in value to a series of companies that were not consolidated into Olympus's balance sheet. The loss was transferred by having these other entities purchase the financial assets for their accounting book cost rather than the fair market value. The funds used by these other entities came from bank borrowings arranged by Olympus. Olympus therefore did not report any gain or loss on the sale.

Many years later, when the accounting rules changed such that Olympus would need to consolidate these outside entities, Olympus engineered a plan to purchase these entities at a price much greater than their value (due to the embedded loss in those entities). Olympus recorded the excess of the purchase price over the fair value as goodwill. At the same time, Olympus overpaid for other acquisitions, apparently paying high "fees" that could be used to further obscure the losses. So, effectively, Olympus kept a liability and loss off of its books for many years (understating liabilities and overstating owners' equity) and when they repurchased the entity and were forced to record the liability, they overstated assets (goodwill) to compensate. As with most accounting games, it came to an end when Olympus finally had to recognize the loss, which they initially did by calling it an impairment loss related to the numerous acquisitions.

We will explore examples of overstating financial position in more detail in Chapter 3.

Managing Earnings

The accounting games discussed till this point involve making the current period or periods look better than they should be. Companies can also manipulate income and expenses between years, making one year look better than it should and the other worse. For example, let's say that a company has a terrific year and expects profits to be much higher than normal, but foresees that this anomaly will not persist. The company may want to smooth out its profits—purposefully lowering this year's profits so they can report higher profits the following year. Perhaps they might do this to make the volatility of earnings look smoother or because this might maximize their bonuses over multiple years. Companies can do this either by setting up reserves or provisions for the future using the accruals and deferrals mentioned earlier.

A simple example of this would be for a company to overestimate the level of doubtful accounts (the amount of accounts receivable that are expected to be uncollectible). In doing so, the company overstates bad debt expense in the current period, reducing net income. In a subsequent period, if earnings are below expectations, they can reverse this accrual (provision) to increase earnings in that period. Of course, the company can also do the opposite—if the earlier period is below expectations, they can underaccrue bad debts to increase earnings and plan on reducing this by accruing more in later years. Sometimes, the problem compounds itself: a small accounting game one year, hoping for a reversal in the future, is exacerbated by the next year's similarly dismal performance, forcing an even bigger accounting game to keep the charade going.

We will explore examples of managing earnings in more detail in Chapter 4.

Overstating Operating Cash Flows

This section focuses on the misclassification of cash flows and the fabrication of current-period cash flows, which may be detrimental to future periods. For example, the company can have a real impact on the current-period cash flow by significantly slowing down payments to suppliers. This gives a boost to current cash flows but will have a negative impact on next period's cash flow. A company can also get a short-term boost to cash flow by selling its accounts receivable at a discount and receiving cash earlier than normal. While neither of these situations is improper, the short-term boost to cash flow should be viewed skeptically since the company is effectively borrowing from the future.

However, the company may try to make cash flow look stronger than it really is by misclassifying cash flows. The cash flow statement is composed of three sections; operating, investing and financing. Analysts would like to see the company generating positive operating cash flow and use this cash flow either to invest for the future (investing) or return this capital to investors or creditors (financing). A company can try to make itself look better by trying to classify cash receipts as operating activities (rather than say financing) or classifying cash payments as investing activities (rather than operating). For example, a company might borrow money from a creditor using accounts receivable as collateral and report this as a sale of the receivables (operating) rather than a borrowing transaction. The difference between an outright sale and a loan is real. In the case of a sale, the buyer should not have recourse against the seller if all of the receivables are not collected. However, in the borrowing transaction, the company is still obligated for any noncollectible accounts.

Another method is to classify a normal operating expenditure as a capital expenditure as described earlier in the Overstating Earnings section. In this manner, operating cash flow is overstated and investing cash flow is understated (larger cash outflows for capital expenditures).

We will explore examples of overstating operating cash flows in more detail in Chapter 5.

Corporate Governance and Related Issues

The themes discussed so far relate to accounting games played to manipulate the financial statements of the company. Another category of problems associated with investing in companies run by others relates to their ability to exert undue influence to benefit or enrich themselves (and sometimes their friends and family) at the expense of other shareholders. We will also include in this category other issues that are not strictly accounting related but should result in a heightened degree of skepticism about the company.

Good corporate governance provides a system in which controls are in place to make sure that the potential for conflicts of interests between insiders (principally management) and external shareholders is appropriately managed. An example of good corporate governance would be a strong slate (majority) of external, independent board members who act in the best interest of shareholders in overseeing the work of management. Good corporate governance also includes a sufficient level of transparency and disclosure such that external investors can best evaluate the financial position of the company and the performance of management. If corporate governance is weak, investors have to raise the level of due diligence they perform when they consider making or continuing an investment in the company. Given the number of investment alternatives that exist, sometimes it is best to avoid companies with poor corporate governance altogether, as the risks can be too high.

We will explore examples of corporate governance and related issues in more detail in Chapter 6.

PARTING COMMENTS

No method to detect fraud is foolproof. Unfortunately, if a company wants to intentionally perpetrate fraud, it can be very hard to detect until it is too late, even for experienced auditors and analysts. With the framework we have established, we hope to provide the basic tools for our readers to spot the warning signs in a company's financials if there is something amiss.

NOTE

1. The primary users of financial statement information are investors and creditors, but many others are also interested in analyzing these financial statements, such as journalists, regulators, attorneys, and students. For simplicity, we will refer to anyone analyzing the financial statements, whatever their capacity, as analysts even though that may not be their profession.

REFERENCES

Muddy Waters Research. 2011. "Report on Sino-Forest Corporation," June 2.

Olympus Corporation, The Third Party Committee. 2011. "Investigation Report: Summary," December 6.

Ontario Securities Commission. 2012. "In the Matter of Sino-Forest Corporation, Allen Chan, Albert Ip, Alfred C. T. Hung, George Ho, Simon Yeung and David Horsley: Statement of Allegations," May 22.

Schilit, Howard, and Jeremy Perler. *Financial Shenanigans: How to Detect Accounting Gimmicks & Fraud in Financial Reports 3rd Edition.* New York: McGraw-Hill, 2010.

United States District Court for the District of Columbia. *U.S. Securities and Exchange Commission v. Satyam Computer Services Limited d/b/a Mahindra Satyam,* April 5, 2011.

CHAPTER 2

DETECTING OVERSTATED EARNINGS

This chapter examines one of the most common goals of unscrupulous managers—overstating profits relative to the underlying reality. The chapter addresses cases that range from aggressive reporting (premature revenue recognition) to outright fraud (reporting nonexistent revenues). The chapter presents real cases of companies that have been accused, but not necessarily ascertained guilty, of manipulating their reported results and provides techniques and warning signs to detect this type of activity.

In this chapter, we explore techniques used by companies to overstate earnings and present some warning signs (so-called red flags) that may alert you to potential problems. In some cases, companies will play games that do not overstate bottom-line earnings (net income) but overstate revenues or some subtotal of earnings such as gross margin or operating margin. These techniques will also be addressed in this chapter.

What motivates a company to overstate earnings? As noted in Chapter 1, both investors and creditors are interested in the level of profits of a company. The higher the earnings or profit, the more can be returned to investors and creditors or invested for the future. If management want to make themselves look better to creditors or investors, they may be motivated to play accounting games to make earnings appear better than they actually are, especially if managers' compensation is linked to earnings or share price.

There are four main types of games played by companies with regard to the income statement as depicted in Exhibit 2.1. We will examine each of these in detail.

23

EXHIBIT 2.1   Income Statement Games

In this and subsequent chapters, we will illustrate the techniques that companies use to play accounting games and the techniques that analysts can use to detect problems through case studies of real companies. Since companies rarely engage in only one game at a time, we will present all of the issues together, even though some of the discussion related to the case will occur in later chapters.

AGGRESSIVE REVENUE RECOGNITION

Aggressive revenue recognition is where a company overstates revenues and earnings by reporting revenue on the income statement earlier than the economics of the transaction or in some cases in the absence of a true transaction—for example, fraudulent reporting of revenue. We will also include in this category the overstatement of gains or understatements of losses.

Generally, revenue is recognized when the company has delivered goods or services to its customers, which could be before or after cash is received. As a result, there is a timing difference between the time when sales transactions are reflected on the income statement and the cash flow statement. Some companies are more aggressive than others when they report revenues on the income statement—sometimes within the range of possibility of accounting standards and sometimes contrary to accounting standards.

Companies are generally required to report their revenue recognition policies in their financial statement footnotes. These should always be examined to determine if a company's policies are consistent with their peers—other companies in the same industry. For example, if two companies are in the computer leasing industry as lessors and Company A structures leases as operating leases where they report income over a multiyear period, while Company B structures leases as capital/sales type leases where they record all of the revenue at the inception of the deal (when the equipment is installed), then Company B is being more aggressive than Company A, even though they may both be following accepted accounting principles. A more extreme example is when a company records the sale once the contract is signed even though they still have an obligation to deliver the equipment and make sure it is working at a later date. This would be more than aggressive, even improper. Further still would be the company that records a sale when no contract has been signed, no goods and services delivered, perhaps where no customer even exists—fraudulent revenue.

Now let's distinguish between revenues and gains/losses. Revenues are gross amounts realized from the sale of goods or provision of services from normal operations. For example, if the company is in the restaurant business, then the full amount received from the sale of meals is reported at the top of the income statement as revenue. Any costs incurred in generating that revenue are listed separately in the operating section of the income statement. Gains and losses are transactions that are related to secondary or peripheral activities and are normally reported on a net basis in the non-operating portion of the income statement (near the bottom). For example, if a restaurant has surplus kitchen equipment that has a remaining cost basis of HKD 80,000 that it does not need and sells to a used equipment dealer for HKD 100,000, then the net HKD 20,000 gain is reported in the non-operating section rather than reporting HKD 100,000 of revenue and separately HKD 80,000 of expense. The distinction is important for the user to evaluate how much of a company's earnings come from sales of goods and services in their primary operating businesses.

Now let us take a look at a simple legitimate cash transaction and how the income statement and balance sheet are impacted. The simplest transaction occurs when a company provides services in exchange for cash. For simplicity, let's also assume that there are no expenses associated with this transaction. Revenue and hence net earnings increase on the income statement, as shown in Exhibit 2.2.

EXHIBIT 2.2   Income Statement Impact of Increased Revenue

Since the revenue is received in cash, there is no difference between earnings and cash flow in this case—the company reports the same amount as cash flow from operating activities. On the balance sheet, cash and retained earnings (part of equity) both increase by the same amount, and the accounting equation remains in balance, as shown in Exhibit 2.3.

How would this differ if this were a legitimate transaction, but instead of receiving cash, the company received a promise to pay within a certain number of days—called an accounts receivable or trade receivable? There is no difference on the income statement. On the balance sheet, there is also no difference on the right-hand side (equity). On the left-hand side, accounts receivable (an asset) would increase rather than cash. In a future period when the customer pays, cash will go up and accounts receivable will go down. Of course, if the customer does not pay, the accounts receivable amount would remain on the balance sheet until the company deems it worthless and then must write it off by reducing accounts receivable and recording a loss on the income statement, which reduces retained earnings and owners' equity.

So when a company is very aggressive at reporting revenue by reporting it too soon or fraudulently on the income statement, this will result in a corresponding misstatement on the balance sheet. Whenever earnings are overstated, retained earnings are overstated on the balance sheet. In order to compensate, the company must either overstate assets, understate liabilities, or understate some other component of owners' equity, as shown in Exhibit 2.4.

EXHIBIT 2.3   Balance Sheet Impact of Increased Revenue

EXHIBIT 2.4   Impact of Overstating Earnings on Balance Sheet

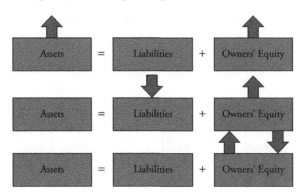

In the case where revenue is overstated, the most likely scenario is the first: assets are overstated. From our basic example it should be obvious that the asset involved is often accounts receivable. In the most extreme cases, the company is reporting fictitious revenue for which no cash is ever collected and the accounts receivable balance grows continuously over time. In other cases, the company may be very aggressive about how it reports revenue and report it before a transaction has taken place or before the revenue is truly earned (e.g., reporting revenue when a contract is signed even though delivery is to occur in the future or the contract relates to use of the asset over time rather than an immediate sale). In such cases, accounts receivable will increase in the current period at a faster rate than it should but would (hopefully) be reconciled in a subsequent period. Since fraudulent behavior is often repetitive, even in these latter cases, the accounts receivable balance will continue to grow at a faster pace relative to what it should.

As a result, most cases of aggressive and fraudulent revenue recognition result in large increases in receivables. This can be detected by looking at the pace of receivables growth over time relative to revenues, examining the days sales in receivables ratio or comparing cash flow from operations relative to earnings for a disconnect between reported revenue and cash received from customers.

Application: Satyam

Recall the example of Satyam in Chapter 1. In Satyam's case, receivables on the balance sheet were increasing at a more rapid pace than revenues: While revenues for the fiscal year ended March 2008 increased by 46 percent, the company's three receivables accounts all increased by a greater extent, with short-term trade receivables increasing by 51 percent, long-term trade receivables increasing by 80 percent, and unbilled revenue (also a receivable) increasing by 111 percent. This is a warning sign of perhaps aggressive or fraudulent revenue recognition, a lowering of credit standards, or a general problem with the company's ability to collect from customers.

A company can also report fraudulent revenue without an overstatement of receivables but has to get more creative. One way to do this is for the company to report a fictitious receipt of cash from customers—lowering accounts receivable and overstating cash reported on the balance sheet. While this may appear unattractive due to the perceived ease with which the company's auditors can detect the nonexistence of such cash, there have been several recent scandals where this has occurred and the overstatement of cash was not detected. For instance, Satyam overstated its cash position through a "special" cash account on its balance sheet called "Investments in Bank Deposits."

Application: Longtop Financial—Cash

Note: Full case study presented at the end of this chapter.

A similar situation occurred recently with Longtop Financial. Longtop's auditors had been confirming cash balances with local branches of the bank where Longtop was located. After a research report was issued suggesting accounting problems were occurring at Longtop, the auditor decided it had better confirm those cash balances with the main offices at the bank. When Longtop found out this plan, it dismissed the auditors. Later, a company official admitted to the audit partner that there was "fake" cash listed on the balance sheet due to prior recording of "fake" revenue. In fact, the cash balance that Longtop listed on its balance sheet accounted for more than half of the company's total assets—certainly something that should not occur for a manufacturing company that typically has the majority of its assets composed of property, plant, and equipment (PP&E).

Over time, companies have come up with other creative ways to reduce the accounts receivables balance that arises from "cooking the books." Sino-Forest's application of this technique is a great example.

Application: Sino-Forest

Note: Full case study presented at end of this chapter.

Sino-Forest created other companies that it effectively controlled. Sino-Forest then engaged in fraudulent purchases and sales of timber. In this manner, both accounts receivable (from fraudulent sales) and accounts payable (a liability for amounts due to alleged suppliers for timber purchases) would have been overstated. Sino-Forest engaged in an additional scheme to offset the receivables and payables between the controlled "customers" and "suppliers." Of course, the offset was not perfect since the sales prices exceeded the purchase prices; as such, increasingly more purchases and sales had to be recorded to keep the scheme going. Additionally, in order for the accounting equation to balance, some asset had to remain overstated. The overall impact of this transaction was to overstate inventory (which it called Timber Holdings and classified as an investment—also a debatable classification, so we will treat it as inventory in this discussion). To summarize the steps and resulting impact on the balance sheet (up arrow designates overstatement and down arrow designates understatement):

Fictitious sale
↑ Accounts Receivable (asset) ↑ Equity
Fictitious purchase
↑ Inventory (asset) ↑ Accounts payable (liability)
Offset accounts receivable and accounts payable
↓ Accounts Receivable (asset) ↓ Accounts Payable (liability)
End result
↑ Inventory (asset) ↑ Equity

Ultimately, it overstated earnings, equity, and inventory. The conclusion you should reach from this is that aggressive or fraudulent revenue recognition should result in an overstatement of some asset, which will help you identify where to look for potential problems. The most likely overstatements of assets in order of likelihood are accounts receivable, cash, inventory, or investments.

UNDERSTATEMENT OR DEFERRAL OF EXPENSES

Another method of reporting higher earnings is to understate expenses or losses either by avoiding reporting them altogether or deferring them to a later period. The impact on the income statement is shown in Exhibit 2.5.

Similar to overstating revenues, which overstates earnings, understating expenses will result in overstated retained earnings (part of equity) and must be offset by either an overstatement of assets, understatement of liabilities, or understatement of another component of equity, as shown earlier in Exhibit 2.4. For instance, where a company sells goods (inventory) and reports the revenue on the income

EXHIBIT 2.5   Understating Expenses or Losses on the Income Statement

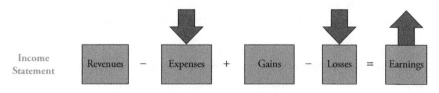

statement but fails to transfer the cost of that inventory to cost of goods sold, earnings and assets in the form of inventory both become overstated. Over time, this results in a large increase in the inventory balance on the balance sheet. Effectively, the company is deferring reporting inventory expenses to a later period.

Other ways of deferring expenses include capitalizing an expense by placing the charge in a balance sheet asset account rather than an expense account on the income statement, for example, misclassifying an expense as property, plant, and equipment (PP&E) or another type of deferred asset. Some companies have created special categories on their balance sheet for these deferred expenses such as "deferred customer acquisition costs." While there are certainly legitimate applications, such as in the insurance industry to account for commissions paid on long-term contracts, this account is often used to avoid reporting marketing expenses on the income statement.

A company could also understate expenses by failing to accrue a liability on the balance sheet. For example, a company may have incurred an expense by contracting for services from a supplier without paying cash when incurred. By failing to accrue (record) the liability and expense, the company would overstate earnings and equity while understating liabilities. When the cash is subsequently paid, the company would necessarily need to record the expense, but may again offset this charge by failing to record liabilities for new expenses incurred. A more sophisticated method could involve a company, Company A, setting up another company, Company B, in such a manner by which Company B is not consolidated with Company A. Some expenses (or losses) could be shifted to Company B so that the earnings of Company A are overstated. Company A would also fail to record the liability for payment of the expenses or loss incurred, even though it may be legally obligated to do so. This technique was recently used by Longtop Financial.

Application: Longtop Financial— Unconsolidated Affiliate

Longtop set up a new company, Xiamen Longtop Human Resources (XLHRS), to employ the majority of the employees of Longtop Financial, which was not consolidated. The company disclosed the following in Securities and Exchange Commission (SEC) filings:

> In addition, as of March 31, 2010, 3,413 of our total 4,258 employees were contracted through third-party human resources companies of which 3,235 were contracted through Xiamen Longtop Human Resources Service Co., Ltd., or XLHRS, which is unrelated to us.

Effectively, employees and expenses related to them were kept "off the books" in another related entity with very low service fees actually paid to XLHRS.

Similarly, a company could avoid recording a loss in other manners as well. For example, if an asset the company owns has declined in value, the company can continue to show it on the balance sheet at the older, higher cost/value. In doing so, the company has overstated earnings, equity, and assets. Conversely, the company may have incurred a loss due to some event or litigation for which it should show a liability on the balance sheet and a loss on the income statement. The company could simply choose not to record the liability or loss, overstating earnings, overstating equity, and understating liabilities.

CLASSIFICATION OF NON-OPERATING INCOME

Many analysts focus on subcomponents of earnings rather than the bottom line—net earnings or net profit. For example, it is common to focus on the company's core business through operating earnings. While it is certainly good to understand how much of a company's profits come from normal recurring operations, we must also understand that companies are aware of this and may try to mislead us. One common ploy of unscrupulous managers is to inappropriately report non-operating gains as part of operating revenues (and do so on a gross rather than net basis) as depicted in Exhibit 2.6. This overstates both revenues and operating earnings but has no effect on the bottom-line net earnings.

CLASSIFICATION OF NON-OPERATING EXPENSES

Another option is to move expenses down the income statement and classify them as a "special" or "extraordinary" loss to make normal operating earnings look larger, as shown in Exhibit 2.7. While accounting standards are quite strict as to what is considered "extraordinary," there is flexibility for management to use other titles such as special charges. You should use your own discretion in evaluating just how special these items are. Many analysts simply reclassify them back into normal operating expenses for analysis purposes.

EXHIBIT 2.6   Shifting Gains on the Income Statement

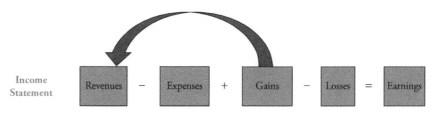

| Income Statement | Revenues | − | Expenses | + | Gains | − | Losses | = | Earnings |

EXHIBIT 2.7   Shifting Expenses on the Income Statement

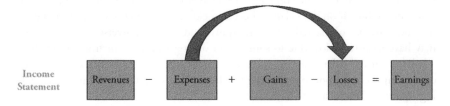

PARTING COMMENTS

We have seen from the discussion and cases in this chapter that there are various accounting games that companies can play to overstate earnings. In fact, overstatement of earnings is the most common reason for a company's undertaking of such games. Fortunately for the analyst, accounting games to increase earnings must have an impact on the balance sheet, which can be detected by comparing earnings reported on the income statement with the cash flow reported on the cash flow statement. Based on the cases presented here and other cases examined by the authors globally, we can synthesize the games down to common themes, which enables us to create a checklist of warning signs and analysis techniques (see Exhibit 2.8) to

EXHIBIT 2.8   Checklist of Warning Signs and Analysis Techniques

Aggressive Revenue Recognition	• Examine revenue recognition policy in footnotes relative to peers. • Are customer receivables growing faster than revenues? • Is operating cash flow significantly lower than accounting earnings? • Did significant revenues occur late in the year?
Understating/ Deferring Expenses	• Are depreciation/amortization periods longer than peer companies'? • Are there any deferred expenses listed as an asset on the balance sheet (other than deferred taxes)? • Are there any unusual assets or unexplained large increases in assets such as inventory, particularly relative to revenues?
Classification of Non-Operating Income	• Were "gains" included in revenue? • Is the company's operating description appropriate? • Were one-time or nonrecurring items included in revenue? • Were any gains or revenue based on revaluation of assets?
Classification of Operating Expenses	• Were any expenses or losses listed as "special," extraordinary, or nonrecurring at the bottom of the income statement? • Are there unusually high margins relative to peers (also applies to deferral of expenses)?

detect potential problems resulting in an overstatement of earnings. In addition to these warning signs, you should also look in general as to whether management has any specific pressures or incentives to increase earnings in the current period.

CASE STUDIES

The following cases examine companies that may have been accused—but not necessarily ascertained guilty—of manipulating their reported results. These cases demonstrate many of the concepts presented in this chapter. Note that some concepts in these cases may be related to concepts covered in other chapters; however, the full case is included for completeness and to demonstrate that there is often a plural nature of accounting manipulation.

Case Study 2.1: Longtop Financial (NYSE: LFT)

Background

- Cayman Islands–registered company (New York Stock Exchange [NYSE]-listed, market cap of US$2.4 billion at its peak) that provides a range of software solutions and services to financial institutions in China.
- Company went public on 24 October 2007, raising nearly US$200 million at an initial per-share offer price of US$17.50. Underwriters were Goldman Sachs, Deutsche Bank, and Jefferies & Co.
- Completed secondary equity offering on 18 November 2009, raising more than US$100 million at a per-share offer price of US$31.25. Underwriters were Deutsche Bank, Morgan Stanley, Janney Montgomery Scott, Kaufman Bros., Macquarie Capital Partners, Needham & Co., and William Blair & Co.
- In the fiscal year ending March 2010, Longtop reported gross margins of 69 percent and non–generally accepted accounting principles (GAAP) operating margins of 49 percent, much higher than peers who reported gross margins between 15 percent and 50 percent and operating margins of 10 percent to 25 percent or even lower.

What Happened

- Citron Research (www.citronresearch.com) released a report on 26 April 2011, highlighting four key allegations of fraud:
  1. Spectacularly high gross margins of 69 percent and operating margins of 49 percent, far in excess of competitors.

2. Staffing model allowed Longtop Financial to transfer the majority of its cost structure off balance sheet to Xiamen Longtop Human Resources (XLHRS), a company that Longtop alleged to be unrelated to.
3. Nondisclosure regarding Longtop's chairman and CEO's former employer, Xiamen Dongnan, who sued them for unfair business practices.
4. Longtop's Chairman transferred 70 percent of stock holdings to employees and friends in the first four years of the company's going public.

- In response to the Citron report, Longtop increased its previously announced share repurchase program by US$50 million, up to a total of US$100 million, on 28 April 2011.
- On 2 May 2011, Longtop's CFO, Derek Palaschuk, announced that he had resigned from his post as head of the audit committee at Renren, which was poised for a heavily anticipated initial public offering (IPO), so that no unwarranted attention would be brought to Renren.
- Citron released another report on 9 May 2011, where it showed that XLHRS was related to Longtop based on legal documentation. The financials of XLHRS, as disclosed in China's State Administration of Industry & Commerce (SAIC), filings also did not match up with the numbers in Longtop's U.S. SEC filings (Form 20-F).
- Longtop announced on 18 May that they would not file their fourth-quarter and fiscal-year financial results on Monday, 23 May 2011. This caused the SEC to halt the trading of Longtop Financial stock on the NYSE on 18 May 2011.
- On 22 May, Deloitte resigned as Longtop's independent audit firm. The resignation was the result of, among other things, falsification of accounting records, the deliberate interference by the company's management in the independent auditor's audit process, and the unlawful detention of the independent auditor's audit files. Deloitte further stated that it was no longer able to place reliance on management's representations in relation to prior-period financial reports.
- On 16 August 2011, the NYSE determined that the shares of Longtop would be suspended from trading before the opening of the trading session on 17 August 2011. The company had a right to appeal the determination to delist its stock but failed to submit an appeal request within the allotted time period.
- On 19 August 2011, Citron released a statement discussing Longtop Financial's (OTC: LGTFY) potential of being a takeover target. Citron mentioned that Longtop provides software solutions to China's largest banks, and their checks show that the company is still operational after it was delisted. They stated that if LGTFY were only "half a fraud," the company could go from its current level of US$0.80/share to between US$4 and $5/share in the near term.
- However, Longtop's shares subsequently fell dramatically.

Longtop Share Price

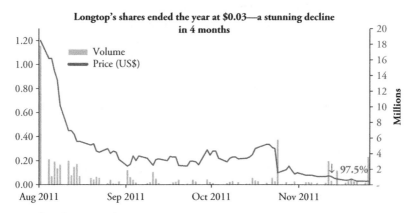

Source: Bloomberg price data.

Warning Signs

- Spectacularly high gross margins of 69 percent and operating margins of 49 percent, far in excess of competitors such as VanceInfo, Camelot, HiSoft, and ISS.
  - Peers reported much lower gross margins of between 15 percent and 50 percent and operating margins of 10 percent to 25 percent or even lower. The discrepancy versus peers is very suspicious in cost-competitive China.
  - Longtop believes that the non-GAAP financial measures provide useful information to both management and investors by excluding certain items that the company believes are not indicative of their core operating results.
  - Management explained the high margins were due to standardizing software sales, claiming that these solutions and modules could be deployed to new customers with fewer man-hours and expenses than peers.
- Staffing model that allowed Longtop Financial to transfer the majority of its cost structure off balance sheet to Xiamen Longtop Human Resources (XLHRS).
  - As of 31 March 2010, Longtop had 4,258 employees, of which 3,413 (80 percent) were employed by third-party human resources staffing companies. Of the employees at staffing companies, 95 percent (3,235) were from a single firm called Xiamen Longtop Human Resources Services Co. (XLHRS), but this entity had no verifiable business presence except for Longtop. (The remaining 5 percent were being serviced by Beijing FESCO and Randstad Shanghai Temp Staffing, both of which do have a verifiable business presence beyond Longtop.)
  - On 26 April 2011, Citron reported that despite Longtop's consistently claiming that XLHRS was an unrelated party, XLHRS contained the Longtop moniker, used the same e-mail server, and occupied the same building as Longtop, which is their only client. XLHRS was formed in May 2007, just

months before Longtop's IPO. XLHRS was never mentioned in the filings until the annual report filed July 2008, even though it is Longtop's largest line expenditure. Further, Longtop did not have any long-term contracts and did not have to pay any penalties or minimums in its relationship with XLHRS. Longtop terminated the outsourcing agency and took all the employees in-house when the outsourcing agency relationship was questioned. XLHRS had no website and did not appear to be soliciting customers even though it had just lost its only customer.

- Longtop claimed that the outsourcing arrangement was part of the justification of its outsized margins. However, after dumping XLHRS, the company claimed that there would be no financial penalty, no cost, and no margin loss associated with terminating the relationship.
- On 9 May 2011, Citron reported that Longtop's legal department staff had been signing off on a variety of administrative filings with the government on behalf of XLHRS, which proves that they are related.
- The financials of XLHRS in the SAIC documents stated total revenues (or service fees) of merely RMB$5.1 million, while Longtop's 20-F stated that XLHRS was to receive a service fee that would amount to RMB$400 to 500 million on a conservative basis. Other SAIC filings also show that XLHRS would be underpaying the government for benefits for Longtop employees.
- Nondisclosure regarding Longtop's chairman's and CEO's legal history.
  - Before founding Longtop, Chairman Jia Xiaogong and CEO Lian Weizhou worked for a company named Xiamen Dongnan Computer Co. (XDCC). This information was left out of their bios in the prospectus, possibly because they were sued by XDCC for unfair business practices.
  - In the lawsuit, they were found liable for drawing salaries from XDCC while working for their own company, Xiamen Dongnan Rongtong Electronic Co. (XDREC), which they set up with two other people on 15 July 1996, unbeknownst to their employer, and allegedly recruited 43 of their co-employees.
  - The suit also alleged that on 15 October 1996, Lian signed a contract with one of XDCC's major clients, but inscribed on the contract that he was working for XDREC instead of XDCC. The two company names sound very similar in both Chinese and English, so it would be likely that the client thought he was signing a contract with XDCC.
  - On 26 November 1996, Jia and Lian allegedly sent a letter to the Xiamen Postal Office stating, "due to our business needs, our address has changed from 5th floor, Huli Information Building to 11th floor, Huanjian Building, Xinzhong Road, Xiamen; please forward all relevant mails to the new address." The new address was a post office box they set up to illegally intercept the mail of their namesake company.
- Longtop's chairman transferred 70 percent of stock holdings to employees and friends in the first four years of the company's going public.
  - Citron believes that this transaction of 9 million shares, valued at over a quarter billion dollars, has an undisclosed "tail." The money might have been used to pay off Longtop's hidden liabilities or generate an undisclosed benefit to Longtop's Chairman Jia.

- This type of transaction undermines the credibility of management, especially when there is no transparency.

- OLP Global's review of Longtop's 20 acquisitions raised significant red flags, as most acquired entities appeared to be unprofitable, with outsized operating expenses relative to the scale of the respective businesses. Other red flags identified include ownership issues and opaque disclosures that made it impossible for investors to independently verify a number of transactions.

Key Lessons

- "Extreme outsourcing" obliterates transparency and is a common characteristic of other stocks in China that have collapsed under findings of fraud. For example, China Media Express claimed that the large advertising sales teams responsible for their huge reported income were outsourced; Duoyuan Global Water and Duoyuan Printing also claimed outsourced distributor networks.
- The outsource maneuver makes it difficult to deconstruct the numbers from an auditing standpoint and makes invisible a lot of metrics that would afford meaningful insight into how the company operates, such as ratios of revenues per employee, costs per employee, and so on. Since the entity appears to be a related party, this arrangement makes very little sense from a business standpoint.
- In cost-competitive China, if margins are spectacularly high, it is probably too good to be true.
- Do not rely on management forecasts of revenue and growth numbers.

Case Study 2.2: Sino-Forest

Background

- Sino-Forest was the largest private forestry operator in China, with 790,000 hectares (ha) of reported forestry assets representing US$2.5 billion of book value.
- The company was formed in 1994 and listed on the Toronto Stock Exchange in 1995 through a reverse takeover of an existing public shell company.
- From 2003 to 2010 the company raised about US$3.0 billion through issuing debt and equity securities.
- Sino-Forest reported strong growth and profit margins: between 2005 and 2010, revenues grew at 42 percent compound annual growth rate (CAGR) to US$1.9 billion and net income grew at 56 percent CAGR to US$395 million, representing a 20.5 percent margin.
- The company's share price increased over 300 percent during that period.
- At the end of May 2011, the company had a listed market capitalization of US$4.5 billion and an enterprise value of US$5.3 billion.
- Sino-Forest had attracted a blue-chip investor base, including Paulson (14 percent), Davis Advisors (11 percent), and Capital Group (4 percent).

What Happened

- Despite Sino-Forest's strong reported performance, there had been doubts surrounding the company's business model.
- The key questions raised include:
  - High earnings before interest, taxes, depreciation, and amortization (EBITDA) margins between 60 percent and 70 percent, despite the apparently low value-add role of the company as agent between buyers and sellers of forest plantations.
  - Opaque business structure where the company did not disclose either the buyers or sellers of the plantations. Management referred to these entities as authorized intermediaries (AIs) and claimed they were a source of competitive advantage for the business.
  - Negative free cash flow generation over the past five years, despite having raised about US$3 billion from the debt and equity capital markets since its inception. The company had never paid any dividends to shareholders.
- On 2 June 2011, a research firm, Muddy Waters, released a report accusing Sino-Forest of massive fraud and of effectively being a Ponzi scheme financed by repeated capital raisings. Stock drops 25 percent before trading is suspended.
- On 3 June 2011, Sino-Forest denies all allegations and sets up an independent review committee. Stock falls a further 64 percent on resumption of trading.
- On 8 June 8, 2011, the Ontario Securities Commission opens an investigation.
- On 21 June 2011, the largest shareholder, Paulson, sells its entire 14 percent stake in the company.
- The chairman and CEO resigned in August 2011 following suspension of the stock by the Ontario Securities Commission on suspicion of securities fraud.
- In December 2011, the company announced it would default on its outstanding bonds.
- The board appointed an Independent Committee to investigate the fraud allegations, which issued an interim report in November 2011 and a final report in January 2012. The report's findings failed to dispel the core questions about the business:
  - Only 18 percent of the company's timber holdings were confirmed by official plantation rights certificates and registered title. Claims on the remaining reported holdings were supported only by transaction records that were not officially recognized documents.
  - No independent verification or confirmation could be obtained on either the valuation of Sino-Forest's timber assets or the revenues the company was supposed to have generated from sales.
  - The relationships between Sino-Forest, the AIs, and suppliers are very close, and their business arrangements might never be independently verified as true arm's-length transactions.
  - James Bowland, one of the directors of the board and one of three members on the Independent Committee, resigned two weeks before the issue of the November interim report.

Key Allegations	Muddy Waters Allegations	Company/Other Research House Rebuttals
Use of authorized intermediaries (AIs)	Use of AIs justified by lack of proper licensing for the company to directly conduct transactions: • Sino did have a wholly owned entity that had the correct license, but this was wound down in 2003 for undisclosed reasons. • Company refuses to disclose identities of AIs, making it impossible to verify revenues. • According to management, the AIs are responsible for paying taxes, so Sino has no official tax receipts to substantiate reported sales.	• Third-party industry reports indicate that obtaining forest plantations for sale is very competitive and non-disclosure is a plausible explanation • AIs may be government-linked entities or may have used less-than-acceptable practices to obtain the plantation rights and do not want their identities to be revealed. • Management did release the name of one AI in 2010, but the agent turned out to be a related party.
Overstatement of forest reserves	Sino reported that it had purchased 200,000 ha of plantation trees in Yunnan: • Checks with Yunnan agent indicates that only 13,000 ha of purchases could be verified. • The other agents that reportedly sold Sino the plantations were thinly capped companies managed by a Sino executive with implausible balance sheets consisting primarily of Sino receivables. • Alleged overstatement of forest reserves by US$800 million.	• Flawed understanding of business process. Sino may only have bought the rights to log the standing timber and not to grow new trees (plantation rights), which the agent might have kept. • Although this would cast doubt on the sustainability of Sino's business a few years later when the existing trees have been logged, the existing standing timber still belongs to Sino and should be counted as reserves. • Sino management announced that they are in the process of getting approvals from municipality authorities to publish the relevant agreements.
Inflated revenues	• Sino's 2010 reported timber sales implies a plantation size 5,600 ha larger than the company's contracted holdings, and exceeds the logging quotas for the relevant areas	• Sales of standing timber do not translate to immediate logging. Customers sometimes wait for a few years for the purchased trees to mature before logging.

- The reports highlighted several key corporate governance issues, including lack of an integrated accounting system, absence of an internal audit function, and an uncooperative management team.
- The Ontario Securities Commission (OSC) filed fraud charges against members of management of Sino-Forest in May 2012.
    - The OSC allegations provide details on fraudulent activities, including double counting of timber sales in multiple subsidiaries and schemes that recycled cash (cash was paid for alleged purchases of timber to related parties and redirected back into Sino-Forest as payment on receivables).

Warning Signs

- Sino-Forest's use of AIs lies at the heart of the allegations, as it allows the company to report sales, purchases, and forest reserves without third-party verification.

Diagram of AI Structure

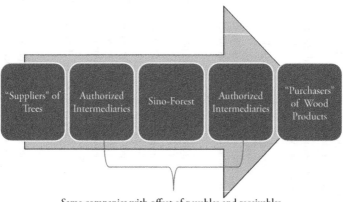

Same companies with offset of payables and receivables

- Despite reporting positive cash flow from operations, cash expenditure on acquisition of timber holdings has consistently outstripped cash flow generation.
- Receivables account has registered significant increases over the past four years, as did investment in timber holdings. As the following table shows, while revenue was up 169 percent from 2007 to 2010, receivables were up over 500 percent and would have been up higher had the company not offset receivables and payables. Note that on a combined basis receivables and timber holdings were up almost 200 percent. Also note the similarity between receivables and payables balances over the four-year period.

	2010	2009	2008	2007	Growth 2007 to 2010
Revenues	1,924	1,238	901	714	169.47%
Receivables	637	282	226	105	506.67%
Timber Holdings	3,123	2,183	1,653	1,174	166.01%
Total	3,760	2,465	1,879	1,279	193.98%
Accounts Payable	500	250	182	108	362.96%

Source: ThomsonReuters.

US$ m	2010	2009	2008	2007
Revenues	1,924	1,238	901	714
Net Income	395	286	229	152
Cash Flow from Opereations before Δ in working capital	1,174	826	542	456
Δ in Accounts Receivable	(346)	(59)	(111)	(24)
Δ in Other Working Capital	12	17	53	7
Net Cash Flow from Operations	840	784	483	486
Additions to Timber Holdings	(1,359)	(1,032)	(657)	(640)
Other Investing Expenditure	(43)	(36)	(47)	(52)
Cash Flow before Financing	(562)	(285)	(221)	(206)

Key Lessons

- In hindsight, there were several red flags that should have alerted investors:
  - Listing through reverse takeover, thus avoiding typical IPO due diligence.
  - Complex and opaque business structure with unidentified counterparty transactions.
  - Consistently negative free cash flow generation.
  - Repeated capital raisings since listing; no return of capital to shareholders.
  - Limited management ownership; chairman owned less than 3 percent of the company.
- Presence of well-known investors no guarantee of safety:
  - Paulson, Davis Advisors, and Capital Group were substantial shareholders pre-allegations.
  - Richard Chandler and Wellington both bought substantial stakes after the allegations were published.

Case 2.3: Oriental Century

Background

- Oriental Century (ORIC) is a provider of education management services to educational institutions in China. The company managed three schools in China, through its principal subsidiary Oriental Dragon Management (ODM), where ORIC received its business revenue.
- The company listed on 1 June 2006, with 33.28 million shares at S$0.35 per share, on the then-SGX-SESDAQ (presently known as Catalist), with a market capitalization of approximately S$12 million.
- Oriental Century seemed to be a profitable, well-run company, where it recorded CAGRs of 38 percent and 56 percent for its revenue and net profit, respectively, from 2002 to 2004.
- In FY2004, ORIC posted pro-forma revenue of RMB42.1 million, gross profit of RMB31.6 million, translating into a gross profit margin of 75.1 percent and net profit margin of 60.6 percent. Operations yielded recurrent cash inflows and had no debt in 2004.
- Two of the schools, Oriental Pearl College and Humen Oriental, are based in Dongguan City, Guangdong. The third, Nanchang Oriental, is in Nanchang City, Jiangxi Province.
- ORIC owned 100 percent of Nanchang Oriental and Humen Oriental through ODM. Oriental Pearl College was owned by Dongguan Baisheng Investments Development (Baisheng).
- The major asset of Baisheng was a piece of land 184,400 sqm located in Dongguan, on which Oriental Pearl College was sited. Baisheng has borrowings that are secured against this land.
- The shareholders of Baisheng were: CEO of ORIC, Yuean Wang 51.5 percent, Zhu Xiaolin (36.5 percent), Zhao Zhong (6 percent), and Ma Xiangdong (6 percent). Zhu Xiaolin was a former nonexecutive director of ORIC, with Zhao Zhong and Ma Xiangdong being senior managers of ODM, the subsidiary of ORIC.
- Raffles Education bought a 29.9 percent stake in Oriental Century in December 2006 and was a passive investor in the company without board or management representation. CEO Chew Hua Seng of Raffles Education believed Oriental Century, as a listed company with its own management, auditors, and governance structure, was a safe investment.
- Oriental Century's auditor was KPMG, and HL Bank was the manager, underwriter, and placement agent for ORIC's IPOs.
- Major shareholders of the company:
  - Raffles Education: 29.9 percent
  - Yuean Wang (CEO): 25.4 percent

- The board of directors were:
  - Leow Poh Chin (nonexecutive director)
  - Lai Seng Kwoon (independent director)
  - Prof. Tan Teck Meng (independent director)

What Happened

- On 24 February 2009, ORIC announced its FY2008 results and stated the company's total cash and cash equivalents were RMB234.4 million as of 31 December 2008.
- Oriental Pearl College reported to ORIC it had a student population of 3,000 students, as of 31 December 2008. Checks conducted by management after March 2009, however, revealed a student population of only 2,200 students.
- CEO Wang had reported to the BOD since 2004 that Nanchang had been profitable since its operations in late 2003, which was reflected in the consolidated accounts of ORIC since 2004.

  However, it was found that Nanchang had been making losses throughout and operated at a student population far below its capacity. In addition, Humen, which started operations in 2008, also reported a loss since it commenced operations, though accounting and related records were falsified to mask true financial performance.
- 12 March 2009: ORIC announced that it had been informed by CEO Wang that the cash initially reported had been substantially inflated. CEO Wang had, over the period from 2004 to 2008, inflated sales and cash balances and diverted unspecified sums to an interested party. Oriental Century's shares were suspended on 9 March 2009, and Yuean Wang was terminated as CEO.
- PricewaterhouseCoopers (PwC) was appointed as special accountant to carry out an independent limited financial review.
- On 2 July 2009, CFO Chan Kheng Hock resigned, and became secretary of ORIC. CIO Lei Hua was appointed as acting CEO on 11 March 2009, though he resigned in December 2009 due to differences in opinions with the board on how ORIC could continue to run its China operations.
- Based on ORIC's annual reports from FY2004 to 2008, the total revenue and accumulated profit-after-tax for the five years were reported to be RMB328.5 million and RMB173 million, respectively. However, during PwC's special audit of the "revised accounts," the total revenue for the same five-year period was only RMB19.9 million, with an accumulated loss of RM55.4 million instead.
- Further investigations by PwC revealed attempts to reconcile the revised accounts versus the reported accounts did not match. This was because PwC was not able to accurately determine the actual number of students in the three schools, as the student population was inflated over the five-year period in order to overstate fee revenue.

- ORIC reported in its annual reports for FY2004 to 2008, that of the RMB328.5 million revenue, RMB212.2 million was from management fees earned by ODM from managing Oriental Pearl College, and RMB114.1 million was revenue from Nanchang Oriental. However, based on bank confirmations obtained by PwC, the total bank balance of ORIC as of 31 December 2008, amounted to only RMB1.8 million versus the RMB234.4 million stated in ORIC's announcement of FY2008. The difference arose from discrepancies in two bank accounts: one from Guangdong Development Bank opened by ODM, and the other in ICBC bank opened by Nanchang Oriental.
- Since the incident of March 2009, the board of directors attempted to sustain the operations of ORIC's subsidiaries in China.
- On 2 December 2010, an emergency meeting was called, and a resolution was passed to have BDO LLP appointed as liquidator for the purpose of winding up ORIC. The company was eventually delisted from Catalist on 30 May 2011.

Warning Signs

Oriental Dragon Management (ODM)

- Of the reported RMB212.2 million earned by ODM from Oriental Pearl College (annual reports FY2004 to 2008), it was revealed by ODM's bank statements that ODM had received only RMB90.3 million for the five-year period.
- Of this RMB90.3 million, RMB83.9 million was paid out by ODM within *one month* to the following parties:
  - Baisheng: RMB9.4 million
  - Oriental Pearl College: RMB8.13 million
  - Shenzhen Julong Investment Development: RMB63.5 million
  - Dongguan City Technology Investment Assurance: RMB2.8 million
      The shareholders of Shenzhen Julong were CEO Wang 28 percent, Zhu Xiaolin 22 percent, Zhao Zhong 10 percent, and Ma Xiangdong 10 percent—all of whom are also shareholders of Baisheng.
- In addition, of RMB46.24 million injected into ODM as capital from Oriental Century, ODM paid out RMB40.1 million within *one month* of receipt to:
  - Baisheng: RMB35.05 million
  - Dongguan City Yuesheng Commercial: RMB5.0 million

Nanchang Oriental

- PwC estimated that total receipts collected by Nanchang for FY2004 to 2008 was approximately RMB70 million. Of this, RMB32 million were from ODM, Baisheng, and Julong, which were unrelated to payment of school fees by students.
      Of the remaining RMB38million of receipts, PwC ascertained that only RMB12.9 million was related to collection of school fees from students. This was in contrast to the RMB114.1 million recorded in Nanchang's accounts, as mainly from school fees collected.

Payments and Receipts for Unknown Purposes

- On review of bank statements of ODM, Nanchang and Dongguan Oriental Dragon (subsidiary of ORIC whose principal activity is investment holding), from FY2003 to 2008, RMB43 million was made by these three subsidiaries to entities outside ORIC.
- In addition, there was approximately RMB41.3 million of receipts from entities outside ORIC for which no adequate supporting documents were given.
- All the transactions mentioned above to the various subsidiaries were not recorded by the respective subsidiaries, nor mentioned in the annual reports.
- There was also no evidence of approval for the payments by the board of directors.

Corporate Governance

- Approvals in the form of two seals for the unrecorded payments from bank accounts were held by an accountant of ODM who was based in Beijing (i.e., finance seal), and CEO Wang (i.e., legal representative seal).
- The remaining three directors (two independent, one nonexecutive) were not informed of the payments.

Key Lessons

- Look beyond the big names of strategic investors (e.g., Raffles Education in this case) and see if they have a board seat in the governance of the company.

  Raffles Education bought its 29.9 percent stake in Oriental Century from two UOB private equity vehicle funds in December 2006, and did not seek a board seat on ORIC. Raffles Education, despite being a savvy investor in the education sector in China, was also deceived by ORIC.
- **Alignment of interest between management and shareholders**

  By using ODM as the vehicle for siphoning cash from Oriental Pearl College, Wang paid out Baisheng and Shenzhen Julong, where he held 51.5 percent and 28 percent stake, respectively. This allowed Wang to enrich himself at the expense of shareholders, as both groups' interest were not the same.

  CEO Wang only owned 25.4 percent stake in ORIC, less than Raffles Education's 29.9 percent. This small quantum of ownership showed a lack of shareholder alignment with the CEO.
- **Scrutiny of corporate governance**

  The shareholders of Baisheng were comprised of two senior managers of *ODM* and a former non-exec director of ORIC, and CEO Wang. Understanding how/why the four men came to own Oriental Pearl College through Baisheng would raise concerns on how ODM would be effectively managed when ODM received management fees from Oriental Pearl College.

REFERENCES

Citron Research reports on Longtop Financial. 2014. www.citronresearch.com, as of 12 January 2014.

Muddy Waters Research. 2011. "Report on Sino-Forest Corporation," June 2.

Norris, Floyd, 2011. "The Audacity of Chinese Frauds," *New York Times*, May 26.

Ontario Securities Commission. 2012. "In the Matter of Sino-Forest Corporation, Allen Chan, Albert Ip, Alfred C.T. Hung, George Ho, Simon Yeung, and David Horsley: Statement of Allegations," May 22.

PricewaterhouseCoopers. 2009. Announcement to Oriental Century Limited shareholders, May 26.

CHAPTER 3

DETECTING OVERSTATED FINANCIAL POSITION

This chapter takes a look at companies that attempt to make their financial position look stronger than it really is. This practice is commonly associated with the overstatement of assets, although that is not necessarily the case. The company may want to understate both assets and liabilities, which improves profitability ratios (such as return on assets) or debt ratios (by making them look smaller). This chapter provides you with the tools and techniques to detect such activity.

While earnings are typically a focus of investors, and company managers have clear incentives to overstate earnings to benefit their compensation, there are also incentives to overstate the company's current financial position. This entails presenting a stronger balance sheet, also known as the statement of financial condition or statement of financial position. The balance sheet is a common focus of creditors and is also of interest to most investors. In fact, common financial ratios used by investors, such as return on assets and return on equity, require balance sheet information and are often a target of management manipulation. As demonstrated in earlier chapters, our view is that all investors should always examine the balance sheet in conjunction with the income statement, as either statement has a corresponding effect on the other. The balance sheet can be represented by the accounting equation shown in Exhibit 3.1.

Overstating financial position involves making a company's balance sheet appear stronger. The most common ploy involves simultaneously keeping both assets and liabilities off the balance sheet entirely—in fact, some accounting rules permit this to occur (e.g., operating leases). This can improve some financial ratios, in particular financial leverage ratios, substantially. Another alternative is to keep liabilities off the balance sheet such as by using off-balance-sheet financing or failing to record a loss incurred. Another ploy is to overstate assets—either those shown on the balance sheet explicitly or off-balance-sheet assets such as commodity reserves. However, overstating balance sheet assets can actually harm some of the company's financial ratios, as we shall see later. The most common types of balance sheet accounting manipulations are depicted in Exhibit 3.2.

If the company wants to understate liabilities, it must either understate assets or overstate owners' equity, as shown in the first and second panels of Exhibit 3.3, in order for the balance sheet to balance. If the company wants to overstate the value of assets presented on the balance sheet, it typically must overstate owners' equity (the only alternative would be to overstate liabilities, which would harm the company's reported financial position, not strengthen it). If a company overstates the value of assets off balance sheet (e.g., reserves of precious metals or oil), there is no balancing effect needed on the balance sheet, so the analyst must examine footnotes and external sources to detect and evaluate the value of these resources.

EXHIBIT 3.1   The Balance Sheet Accounting Equation

EXHIBIT 3.2   Common Balance Sheet Accounting Games

EXHIBIT 3.3   Balance Sheet Impact

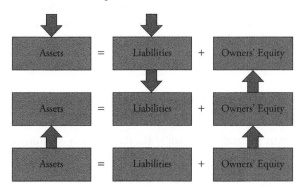

EXCLUDING BOTH ASSETS AND LIABILITIES

Excluding both assets and liabilities from the balance sheet is the easiest technique to employ, and current accounting rules permit some ways of achieving this result. It may seem strange that a company would want to understate assets, as assets are normally thought of as a good thing—a resource the company has control over to benefit operations. However, if a company wants to understate its liabilities, an easy way to accomplish this given the nature of the accounting equation is to also understate assets. Understating assets also improves some financial ratios – most importantly return on assets. Return on assets is a measure of profitability where a higher number is preferable to a lower number. It is typically computed as net earnings divided by total assets. By understating assets, the company's return on assets will be higher.

Let's first address a legitimate way that companies can get the benefits of the use of assets without having to show the asset and a corresponding obligation (liability) on the balance sheet. The technique that companies use is leasing. Currently, under both International Financial Reporting Standards (IFRS) and U.S. generally accepted accounting principles (GAAP), companies that engage in operating leases are not required to put the corresponding asset or liability on the balance sheet.[1] In an operating lease, a company is renting the asset from another party for a periodic payment. The lease could be long term or short term; however, in some circumstances for longer-term leases where the transaction economically resembles a purchase, the accounting rules would require recording of an asset and liability (called a capital or financing lease). By leasing the asset using an operating lease, the company gains use of the asset without reflecting it as a liability on the balance sheet. This is effectively an off-balance-sheet financing, which results in better return on assets and debt-to-equity ratios versus what would be shown if the asset had been purchased and financed. Even though this is permitted under accounting rules, analysts should carefully consider the impact of leasing on the balance sheet and ratios—particularly when you are comparing one company to another. Analysts can adjust the companies' reported financial statements to see what the impact would have been if the asset had been purchased. Two industries in which the use of operating leases is prevalent globally are retailing and airlines.

Application: Off-Balance-Sheet Assets through Leasing

Retailer A owns its retail stores while Retailer B leases its stores from other entities. Summary financial data from the reported financial statements are as follows:

	Total Assets	Total Liabilities	Net Earnings
Retailer A	HKD 800 million	HKD 400 million	HKD 40 million
Retailer B	HKD 500 million	HKD 200 million	HKD 30 million

Without considering the use of operating leases by Retailer B the analyst would compute the following ratios:

	Liabilities/Asset	Return on Assets
Retailer A	50%	5%
Retailer B	40%	6%

Retailer B looks less risky (lower level of debt relative to assets) and more profitable (higher return on assets).

The footnotes for Retailer B reveal the following information:

Future Operating Lease Payments

Year 1	HKD 30 million
Year 2	HKD 30 million
Year 3	HKD 30 million
Year 4	HKD 30 million
Year 5	HKD 30 million
Cumulative total for years after year 5	HKD 90 million

The analyst estimates that Retailer B has an implicit borrowing rate of 10 percent and a tax rate of 30 percent.

Based on this information the analyst can estimate that the company is obligated to make HKD 30 million in payments for a total of eight years. The present value of these payments is approximately HKD 176 million (assuming beginning-of-year payments for conservatism). If the company had purchased the stores and financed them at 10 percent, it would have additional assets and liabilities of HKD 176 million, and its debt ratio would have been about 56 percent.

To adjust return on assets for Retailer B, you must adjust earnings by adding back the after-tax lease payments and subtracting an estimate of after-tax interest and depreciation expense:

Unadjusted net income	30
Add back after-tax lease expense	21
Subtract after tax interest (17.6 × 0.7)	(12.3)
Subtract after tax depreciation ((176/8) × 0.7)	(15.4)
Adjusted net income	23.3
Adjusted return on assets	4%

After adjustments, Retailer B is riskier and has lower profitability.

Another method of understating both assets and liabilities involves shifting accounts receivable (assets) off the balance sheet in a borrowing transaction. If a company sells its receivable to another entity at a discount for cash (called factoring) and the other entity has no recourse if it fails to collect, then this is a legitimate sale of receivables. Receivables are replaced on the balance sheet with cash. However, if a company borrows money against those same receivables and continues to bear the credit risk of collections, then the receivables stay on the balance sheet and a loan is recorded. Some companies attempt to make a borrowing transaction look like a sale and hence understate assets (accounts receivable) and liabilities (the loan). This is sometimes accomplished through the use of special-purpose entities to permit sale treatment under accounting standards.[2]

Both techniques (leases and sale of receivables) effectively involve off-balance-sheet financing of assets where the obligation and asset are not recorded.

Companies have engaged in a variety of similar techniques to keep assets and liabilities off of the reported balance sheet. This is done by having the assets and liabilities held by another entity that is not consolidated with the reporting company and can include any asset type but is often for large amounts such as property, plant, and equipment (PP&E). This can sometimes be accomplished by using the equity method of accounting permitted by accounting standards in the case of joint ventures and some circumstances where the reporting company does not have a controlling interest (e.g., owns less than the majority of shares). In other cases, the company may simply violate accounting standards and keep the assets and associated liabilities hidden from shareholders and auditors by failing to record them on the balance sheet. Unfortunately, the accounting equation permits this type of misstatement (it remains in balance with an equal amount of assets and liabilities omitted) and is not helpful in uncovering the activity. The analyst must scrutinize the footnotes, news articles, and other sources for evidence that a company is keeping assets and obligations off of its balance sheet. Common terms to look out for in footnotes and news articles are the equity method of accounting, special-purpose entities, joint ventures, associated companies, nonconsolidated entities, guarantees, and commitments.

Another sign would be a lack of sufficient assets on the balance sheet to support the reported operations of the business. Let's take a look at a real example.

Application: RINO International Corp.

RINO International was previously a Nasdaq-listed company based in Dalian, China, involved in wastewater treatment equipment. In November 2010, Muddy Waters Research (www.muddywatersresearch.com) issued a report alleging fraud at RINO. A full case study including an organizational chart and financial data are presented in Case 3.1 at the end of this chapter.

Among other issues, Muddy Waters pointed out that the company controlled a variable-interest entity, which in turn owned three other entities. The company did consolidate these four variable-interest entities, which is where virtually all of the reported property and equipment was held. In spite of the consolidation, the balance sheet presented had a very small number of tangible assets relative to what would be expected for a manufacturer of this size. PP&E accounted for only 4.7 percent of total assets in 2009 and 11.13 percent in 2008 (the company raised significant capital sitting in cash in

2009). Further, both the cash flow statement and balance sheet show that the company did not add property and equipment in 2009 in spite of a 38 percent increase in revenue. Finally, the ratio of revenue to property and equipment (turnover) was as follows:

	2009	2008
Revenue	$192,642,506	$139,343,397
Property and equipment	$12,265,389	$13,197,119
PPE turnover (Rev/PPE)	15.7 times	10.6 times

The company has far less reported property and equipment than other similar manufacturing companies—in particular relative to revenues. This points to either further unreported assets being utilized or fictitious revenue. The Muddy Waters report alleged that it was unable to confirm the companies that were listed as major customers of RINO, which is a strong indicator that the reported revenues may not be real.

OTHER OFF-BALANCE-SHEET FINANCING/LIABILITIES

A company may also try to understate liabilities without having an impact on assets. In this case, in order for the accounting equation to balance, they would also need to overstate owners' equity. This could involve failing to record a liability that would also result in an expense (overstating earnings and owners' equity). For example, the company may know that it has a liability related to an environmental loss and fail to record either the liability or the loss, overstating earnings on the income statement and the company's financial position (understating liabilities and overstating owners' equity). Alternatively, the company might find a creative way of borrowing funds but reflect these in the financial statements as revenue/earnings rather than as a liability (also understating liabilities and overstating owners' equity). A company may have also guaranteed a debt of others and failed to record this liability on its balance sheet or in its footnotes if the liability is a contingent liability. Olympus is a case in which the company failed to record a loss that occurred due to a decline in value of financial assets.

Application: Olympus Off-Balance-Sheet Loss

As noted in Chapter 1, Olympus Corporation incurred a loss in the early 1990s due to a decline in the value of financial assets. Rather than recognizing the loss recording the decline in value directly on the balance sheet of Olympus, the financial assets and a corresponding amount of bank borrowing were effectively transferred to another entity that was not consolidated. Eventually, the company was forced to consolidate this entity and had to play additional accounting games to disguise the loss. The full case is presented at the end of this chapter.

OVERSTATING ASSETS

This category can include overstating the value of an asset or reporting an asset that does not exist. It might also involve a company's overstating the value of "assets" that are not currently reported on the balance sheet. The latter is preferred, as overstating assets that are reflected on the balance sheet may harm certain financial ratios such as return on assets. In some circumstances, assets are effectively overstated due to hiding a loss off balance sheet, such as in the case of Olympus. Overstatement of assets is often associated with an overstatement of earnings as described in Chapter 2—for example, when a company defers an expense by adding the amount to an asset account. In this section, we focus on overstatement of assets to artificially strengthen the financial position (balance sheet) irrespective of whether this results in an overstatement of earnings.

The overall assets of a company are a function of the quantity of assets controlled and the valuation of those assets. An overstatement can therefore involve overstating the quantity of assets or overstating the valuation of those assets. Quantity is easier to verify, so most accounting schemes involve the valuation of assets.

Overstating Valuation of Assets on the Balance Sheet

In the past, assets were largely recorded at some measure of their adjusted cost—typically at cost, and then adjusted over time for an estimate of the decline in value due to use of the assets, called depreciation or amortization. Today, however, accounting standards use a mixed model where many assets are reported at an estimate of their current fair value rather than cost. Exhibit 3.4 shows how International Financial Reporting Standards treat assets currently.[3] The fact that

EXHIBIT 3.4   International Financial Reporting Standards Treatment of Assets

Asset	Valuation	Where Gain or Loss on Change in Value Is Reported
Property, plant, and equipment	Choice of cost model or revaluation model	• Losses reported on the income statement and retained earnings. • Gains reported in other comprehensive income in owners' equity rather than the income statement.
Investment property (land or buildings held for investment as opposed to current use)	Choice of cost model or fair value model	• Gains and losses reported on the income statement and retained earnings.
Intangible assets	Choice of cost model or revaluation model	• Losses reported on the income statement and retained earnings. • Gains reported in other comprehensive income in owners' equity rather than the income statement.
Financial assets (investments in securities)	Fair value or amortized cost depending on type of security (fair value in most cases)	• Gains and losses may be reported in either the income statement or other comprehensive income depending on classification.
Agricultural and biological assets	Fair value less expected cost to sell until harvest	• Gains and losses are reflected on the income statement over time as the assets grow.

valuation can be subjective provides management with opportunities to overstate the value.

PP&E are initially recorded at cost upon acquisition. Subsequently, the company can then choose whether to measure the asset under either a cost model or a revaluation model. The revaluation model is designed for those assets for which a fair value can be measured reliably. For the cost model, the company maintains the original cost, which is adjusted periodically for depreciation or impairments. For the revaluation model, the asset is reported on the balance sheet at its current fair value. If the value declines, the balance sheet is balanced by having the loss reported on the income statement and included in retained earnings—assets go down and owners' equity goes down. If the value increases, the gain is reported in other comprehensive income—a holding account that is part of owners' equity on the balance sheet. This permits the balance sheet to balance since the gain is not reported on the income statements.[4] In the case of property held for investment, there is a similar choice of a cost of fair value model. If the fair value model is chosen for investment property, then all gains and losses are reported in the income statement and hence retained earnings.

Intangible assets are initially recorded at their acquisition costs. Subsequently, the company may report these assets using either a cost model or revaluation model. Under the cost model, adjustments are made for any amortization or impairment in future years. Under the revaluation model, they are reported in the future at fair value, with gains and losses treated similarly to PP&E.

Investments in financial assets (e.g., securities) are initially recorded at their fair value. In subsequent periods, these assets are reflected on the balance sheet at either fair value or amortized cost. Specific criteria are provided to determine which model to use. In order to use the amortized cost model, the asset must be held in a business unit, where the objective is to hold assets to collect contractual cash flows consisting of principal and interest due on specified dates. Otherwise, it is measured at fair value. Gains and losses from changes in value are reported in the income statement unless they are related to securities held for hedging or where the company has elected to report the gains and losses in other comprehensive income (available only for equity investment not held for trading).

Perhaps the most interesting category is agricultural (biological) assets—living plants and animals. Generally, these assets are required to be recorded at fair value less expected costs to sell during the growth, degeneration, production, and procreation period—up to the point of harvest. As a result, fair value would generally increase over time as crops or cattle grow. Gains and losses from changes in fair value over time are reflected in net income and retained earnings. Fair value is not used where it may not be measured reliably. This treatment is thought to better reflect the underlying economics by matching the income with the periods of growth rather than reporting all of the income in the year of harvest; an example given by standard setters would be trees that take 30 years to grow. In the absence of this standard, income would not be reported for the first 30 years.

Application: Oceanus

While the theory behind the accounting for biological assets is sound, it opens the door to management manipulation. It can be difficult to measure the periodic growth of some biological assets, and management may make estimates based on how much income they would like to report in the current year. Oceanus is a Singapore-listed food supplier specializing in the farming, processing, and sale of abalone. The following information was extracted from the company's 2010 annual report:

RMB Thousands	2010	2009	Change
Gain on biological assets	583,422	651,406	−10.44%
Sales of processed marine products	131,533	29,922	339.59%
Sales of food and beverage	71,341	36,306	96.50%
Total	786,296	717,634	9.57%
Profit before income tax	232,827	412,318	−43.53%
Biological assets on balance sheet in thousands of RMB	1,154,580	831,000	38.94%
Purchases of biological assets in thousands of RMB	71,272	65,378	9.02%
Biological assets as a percentage of total assets	50.30%	38.80%	
Quantities of abalones (thousands of units)	178,358	119,775	48.91%
Value per unit RMB	6.47	6.94	−6.70%

The majority of the company's revenue came not from selling abalones but from the growth in the abalones being farmed. In 2011, the company reported a loss in thousands of RMB of 367,435 from "mortality of biological assets" plus a loss in thousands of RMB of 422,806 from a decline in fair value of biological assets. This raises suspicions about the reported "growth" and valuation reported in prior years.

Valuation of marketable securities is relatively easy. Other asset values, however, are subjective. Valuation of land and buildings may not be readily available but can be estimated reasonably well with appraisals. Appraisals are not as easy to get on PP&E, and even less so on intangibles. Valuation of biological assets requires both a good measure of the stage of growth and a value for that stage of growth. The latter may be difficult to obtain if no intermediate market exists for the stage the asset is in.

To evaluate whether a company is potentially playing games with asset valuation, you must first examine the footnotes on accounting policies. If the company is using the fair value method for assets, then it is possible that management might manipulate those values and you must then assess the likelihood that this is happening. The risk is higher for those assets like biological assets where reliable values are harder to obtain than for assets like marketable securities where objective measures of value are more likely to exist. Since details are generally not available for individual asset values, in order to assess how aggressively the company is valuing the assets, you can look to other firms in the same industry to see if valuation levels and changes (gains and losses) are consistent for the industry. In the case of financial assets like securities, you can compare changes to market returns.

Overstating the Quantity of Assets on the Balance Sheet

Companies may try to overstate their overall assets by claiming to have more assets than they do. This is particularly true for assets like inventory, where there may be many items that may be hard to observe. Often, this is associated with an overstatement of income by understating costs of goods sold. As noted in Chapter 2, this can be detected by examining the increase in inventory relative to the increase in revenues. In the case of commodities, companies may also overstate the value of their inventories, not to understate cost of goods sold, but simply to appear as though they have more resources that can be used to generate future revenues. You must generally rely on the auditors to provide comfort that the quantity of such inventory is reasonable, but given the imperfections of the audit process, it is useful to do your own reasonableness tests. For example, in the case of natural resources or other commodities, is the amount of inventory and reserves reported consistent with the company's productive capacity, investments in land/mines, and other companies operating in the same industry and geography?

Overstating Off-Balance-Sheet Assets

In the case of natural resources, the company may have ownership or control over reserves that are not yet formally listed on the balance sheet and that are not even observable—for example, underground reserves of oil or other commodities. These represent potential future assets and revenues for the company, and the company therefore has an incentive to overstate their quantity and/or value to make their financial position appear stronger, even though they are not yet added to the balance sheet. This is easy to do since the quantities are not observable and since this game does not require the balance sheet to balance (these assets do not even appear on the balance sheet).

Furthermore, the company may be able to defer expenses by overstating these reserves. Many expenditures related to discovery and production of these resources are capitalized and amortized over the productive capacity/quantity of reserves. Different countries have different conventions about how exploration expenses may be expensed or capitalized. Indeed, in the United States, oil and gas companies can chose between two different methods, so it is important to read the footnotes to the accounts to understand which method a company is following. By overstating future reserves relative to current production, the company can defer amortization to the future. You should be very skeptical about company estimates of assets such as this, as well as for biological assets. In most jurisdictions, it is required to get an independent estimate for proved reserves ahead of certain capital raises. However, there often is not a requirement to do so on an ongoing basis, though some companies may choose to do so. Finally, the firms that certify reserves are not all the same, and it is important to understand the reputation of the firm that has certified the reserves in question.

Application: Bre-X

A classic example of this type of fraud was Bre-X, a Canadian company with an alleged gold mine in Busang, Indonesia. This was a "penny" stock whose price soared to C$286 per share after announcing significant reserves of gold (70 million troy ounces). The price subsequently collapsed after it was discovered that the gold did not exist. While Bre-X was an outright fraud, other examples are companies that are aggressive in their reserve estimates. An example is Shell Oil, which slashed its proven oil reserve estimates by 20 percent after it was questioned by regulators about reserves not claimed by other oil companies who partnered in the same projects.

Exxon and Chevron, Shell's partners in its Barrow Island project off the west coast of Australia, were conservative in not counting the island's reserves at the time (early 2000s) due to the area's "protected" classification and uncertainty. While the companies have more recently received approval to develop these reserves, Shell's reporting of its reserves at the time was excessively aggressive.

PARTING COMMENTS

We have seen from the discussion and cases in this chapter that there are various accounting schemes that companies can manipulate to overstate their financial position. These are excluding assets and liabilities from the balance sheet, off-balance-sheet financing, and overstating assets. Based on the cases presented here and other cases examined by the authors globally, we can synthesize the games down to common themes, which enable us to create a checklist of warning signs and analysis techniques (see Exhibit 3.5) to detect potential problems resulting in an overstatement of financial position.

EXHIBIT 3.5   Checklist of Warning Signs and Analysis Techniques for Overstating
Financial Position

Exclusion of Assets and Liabilities	• Is the company using operating leases to a greater extent than similar companies?
	• Is the company using the equity method of accounting for affiliates? How would their financials look if these affiliates were consolidated?
	• Has the company shifted accounts receivable off the balance sheet in a transaction that would be better classified as borrowing?
	• Does the company have insufficient assets on its balance sheet to support reported operations and revenues—particularly relative to other, similar companies?
Off-Balance-Sheet Liabilities/ Financing	• Are there financing or guarantee arrangements disclosed in the footnotes of press articles that are not reflected on the balance sheet?
	• Are there discussions about contingencies or losses that are not currently reported on the income statement and for which no current liability is accrued?
Overstating Assets	• Does the company have significant assets that are subject to estimates or assumptions or where objective valuations are not available?
	• Does the company have unusual changes in the quantity or valuation of intangible assets, commodities or biological assets (whether reported on the balance sheet or not)?
	• Were any gains or revenue based on revaluation of assets, and what percentage of operating income comes from these activities?

CASE STUDIES

The following cases examine companies that may have been accused—but not necessarily ascertained guilty—of manipulating their reported results. These cases demonstrate many of the concepts presented in this chapter. Note that some concepts in these cases may be related to concepts covered in other chapters; however the full case is included for completeness and to demonstrate that there is often a plural nature of accounting manipulation.

Case Study 3.1: RINO International Corp. (Nasdaq:RINO)

Background

• Nasdaq-listed company based in Dalian, China, with a market cap of US$444.0 million as of 10 November 2010.

- Designs, manufactures, installs, and services proprietary and patented wastewater treatment, flue-gas desulfurization (FGD) equipment, and high temperature anti-oxidation systems for iron and steel manufacturers.
- Claims to be the market leader in selling FGD and other environmental equipment to Chinese steel mills. FGD sales account for 60 percent to 75 percent of the company's revenue.
- 10 November 2010: Muddy Waters released a research report on RINO, alleging that the company was a fraud. This caused RINO shares to plunge from US$16.27 per share on 9 November to US$10.57 per share on 11 November. Shares of RINO traded as high as US$32.35 per share in 2009.
- Beneficial ownership as of 31 March 2010:
  ZouDejun (director and CEO): 58.32 percent
  MOG Capital, LLC: 7.52 percent
  QiuJianping (director and chairman of the board, wife of ZouDejun): 6.26 percent
- Auditor: Frazer Frost, LLP (successor entity of Moore Stephens Wurth Frazer and Torbet, LLP)

What Happened

10 November 2010:

- Muddy Waters accused RINO of being a fraud and issued a strong sell rating with a US$2.45 price target. The following allegations were made against RINO:
  1. Fabrication of a significant number of FGD system customer relationships. FGD system sales are RINO's largest revenue component, accounting for about 60 percent to 75 percent of revenues.

     RINO disclosed 24 FGD customers in its 2008 and 2009 form 10-Ks and 10 March 2010 investor presentation. Muddy Waters spoke with knowledgeable people at nine of these purported customers. Five of the nine denied having purchased FGD systems from RINO, and it is likely that RINO fabricated a sixth customer relationship. Only three customers confirm having purchased FGD systems from RINO.
  2. RINO's 2009 SEC filings reported revenue of US$192.6 million, while its 2009 China State Administration of Industry and Commerce (SAIC) filings showed revenue of only US$11.1 million. While it is plausible that RINO understated its revenue with the SAIC, not uncommon among Chinese companies, Muddy Waters believes that the firm's SAIC filings were closer to reality—generating less than US$15 million in revenue annually.
  3. RINO's value-added tax (VAT) payment disclosures in its SEC filings contradict its reported revenues.
  4. Lack of diligence by auditor Frazer Frost—RINO claimed that it had no People's Republic of China (PRC) income tax expense in 2008 and 2009,

which was not true and shows significant misstatements in its financials. RINO consistently misstates the PRC tax code, and the explanations of its tax treatment are inconsistent with one another.

5. Muddy Waters believes that RINO is merely a shell company. RINO's CEO, Mr. Zou, and chairwoman, Ms. Qiu, the married couple who founded the business, are blatantly violating agreements by failing to make any required transfers of assets and income from the variable-interest entity (VIE) to RINO. They own 100 percent of the VIE (Dailan RINO) as shown here.

RINO ORGANIZATIONAL CHART

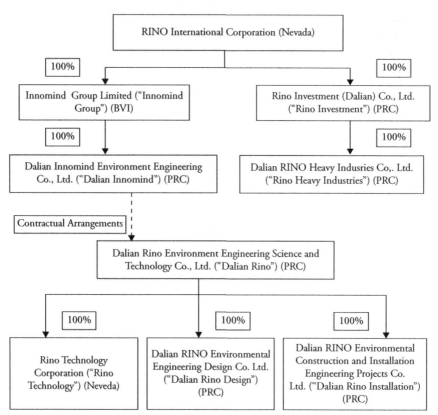

• Under the VIE agreements, the VIE is supposed to sell all of its manufacturing equipment and tangible assets to Innomind (owned by RINO), lease all of its manufacturing plant and land to Innomind, and pay to Innomind on a monthly basis whatever pretax profit the VIE generates.

- However, the VIE is still carrying out all of RINO's operations, and it has not made any management fee payments to Innomind (owned by RINO). Hence, RINO is merely a shell company—RINO's shareholders own little to no productive assets and have received no benefit from the profits the VIE purportedly generates.

  Instead, Mr. Zou and Ms. Qiu have pulled out US$35 to $40 million from Innomind (owned by RINO).

- The VIE reported $156.5 million payable to RINO, but RINO's reported cumulative pretax income from 30 Sep 2007, onward is $120 million. The $36.5 million difference is likely due to the VIE's borrowing money from Innomind.

6. RINO's balance sheet has a very small number of tangible assets for a manufacturer. Instead, it is filled with low-quality "paper" assets.

7. RINO is not the industry leader it claims to be in the steel sinter FGD system industry. Rather, it is an obscure company in a crowded market, yet it claims gross margins of 35 percent to 40 percent on FGD projects, far in excess of leading companies in the industry that generally report less than 20 percent gross margins.

8. Mr. Zou and Ms. Qiu "borrowed" US$3.5 million interest free on the same day that RINO closed its roughly US$100 million financing. On 7 December 2009, RINO completed its registered direct offering with several institutional investors for 3,252,032 shares of its common stock at a price of $30.75 per share, receiving net proceeds of approximately $94.9 million from the offering, after deducting underwriting discounts and estimated offering expenses. In addition to the issuance of the common shares, RINO issued to each investor two warrants exercisable for common shares worth up to approximately an additional $78.5 million in the aggregate, with an exercise price of $34.50 per share. The Series A warrants expired on 7 June 2010, and were immediately exercisable. The Series B warrants expired on 8 December 2010, and were exercisable beginning on June 8, 2010. The offering was underwritten by Rodman & Renshaw, LLC. RINO anticipated that the proceeds from this transaction would be used for working capital requirements. Two days later, the couple purchased a luxury home in Orange County, California, assessed at US$3.2 million.

17 November 2010

- RINO's common stock was suspended from trading on Nasdaq.

8 December 2010

- Delisting of RINO's common stock from Nasdaq.
- RINO resumed trading in the pink sheets, and the stock price quickly fell to $3.15.

2010 year-end

- Various class-action suits were filed against RINO (by Hagens Berman Sobol Shapiro LLP, Pomerantz Haudek Grossman & Gross LLP, Milberg LLP, and Rigrodsky & Long, PA, among others).

3 April 2010

- Chinese media reported that there was an ongoing investigation into a "fraud school" that prepared fraudulent companies to list in the United States via reverse takeovers of public shell companies.
- The article states that this fraud school was responsible for bringing RINO to the United States and that the Chinese investment bank at the center of the fraud school previously worked with American Lorain Corporation, Lihua International, and Fushi Copperweld Inc.

Warning Signs

- The company's business description in its 2009 U.S. Securities and Exchange Commission (SEC) filing Form 10-K begins with "[t]hrough our contractually controlled affiliates in the People's Republic of China. . . ." Throughout the 10-K, it is apparent that the operating assets are not owned by the reporting company but that the reporting company has contracts permitting it to operate the four main operating entities. In fact, the company diagrams this fact in the Form 10-K replicated in the following organizational chart:

RINO INTERNATIONAL CORPORATION AND SUBSIDIARIES
CONSOLIDATED BALANCE SHEETS AS OF 31 DECEMBER 2009
AND 2008

	2009	2008
Assets		
Current Assets		
Cash and cash equivalents	$134,487,611	$19,741,982
Restricted cash	—	1,030,317
Notes receivable	440,100	2,157,957
Due from shareholders	3,005,386	—
Accounts receivable, trade, net of allowance for doubtful accounts of $273,446 and $0 as of December 31, 2009 and 2008, respectively	57,811,171	51,503,245

	2009	2008
Costs and estimated earnings in excess of billings on uncompleted contracts	3,258,806	—
Inventories	5,405,866	1,203,448
Advances for inventory purchases	34,056,231	21,981,669
Other current assets and prepaid expenses	629,506	517,847
Total current assets	239,094,677	98,136,465
Property, Plant, and Equipment, Net	12,265,389	13,197,119
Other Assets		
Advances for non-current assets	6,570,378	6,082,608
Intangible assets, net	1,144,796	1,211,608
Total other assets	7,715,174	7,294,216
Total assets	$259,075,240	$118,627,800
Liabilities and Shareholders' Equity		
Current Liabilities		
Accounts payable	$4,281,353	$5,816,714
Short-term bank loans	1,467,000	8,802,000
Customer deposits	4,984,801	3,609,407
Liquidated damages payable	20,147	2,598,289
Other payables and accrued liabilities	496,411	746,267
Due to shareholder	—	596,023
Taxes Payable	4,003,709	5,062,901
Total current liabilities	15,253,421	27,231,601
Warrant Liabilities	15,172,712	—
Redeemable Common Stock ($0.0001 par value, 5,464,357 shares issued with conditions for redemption outside the control of the company)	24,480,319	24,480,319
Commitments and Contingencies Shareholders' Equity		
Preferred Stock ($0.0001 par value, 50,000,000 shares authorized, none issued and outstanding)	—	—

(*Continued*)

RINO INTERNATIONAL CORPORATION AND SUBSIDIARIES
CONSOLIDATED BALANCE SHEETS AS OF 31 DECEMBER 2009
AND 2008 (Continued)

	2009	2008
Common Stock ($0.0001 par value, 10,000,000,000 shares authorized, 28,603,321 shares and 25,040,000 shares issued and out-standing as of December 31, 2009 and 2008)	2,860	2,504
Additional paid-in capital	107,135,593	25,924,007
Retained earnings	78,983,794	28,570,948
Statutory reserves	11,755,312	6,196,478
Accumulated other comprehensive income	6,291,229	6,221,943
Total shareholders' equity	204,168,788	66,915,880
Total liabilities and shareholders' equity	$259,075,240	$118,627,800

Key Lessons

- Be wary of investing in Chinese companies with VIE structures—if the VIE does not adhere to the contractual agreements it has made with a subsidiary of the listed company, cash that is generated at the VIE might remain in the VIE instead of going to the listed company.
- Compare levels of assets for a company, particularly property and equipment, relative to other, similar companies and relative to the level of reported revenues.

Case Study 3.2: Olympus

Background

- Olympus is a Japanese manufacturer of camera and medical imaging equipment.
- The company generated revenues US$10.6 billion and net income of US$92 million for the year ended March 2011, and had a market capitalization of US$8.2 billion as of 30 September 2011.
- In October 2011, the Board removed the CEO, who had only been appointed in early October.
- The CEO had alleged that the existing management had significantly overpaid for acquisitions and had paid out excessive advisory fees.
- The board appointed an independent committee to investigate the allegations, and it was disclosed in December that the company had used the acquisitions to mask financial losses stemming from investments made in the 1990s.

- Olympus was forced to restate earnings, resulting in a US$1.1 billion cut in net assets; goodwill was reduced from ¥168billion (US$2.2 billion) as of 30 June 2011, to ¥122 billion (US$1.6 billion).

Date	Event
14 October	• Olympus fires CEO Michael Woodford after he questions payments for acquisitions.
21 October	• Company announces it will appoint a third-party committee to conduct investigation into CEO allegations.
26 October	• Chairman/President steps down but retains seat on board of directors. • SEC begins investigation.
8 November	• Announces unreported losses dating back to 1990s, and that acquisition payments appear to have been used to cover up losses.
6 December	• Releases third-party investigative report. • Company placed under Tokyo Stock Exchange (TSE) supervision list for potential delisting.
14 December	• Olympus files five years of corrected financial statements.
20 January	• TSE confirms Olympus will not be delisted, fines company ¥10 million (US$0.1 million).

What Happened

- A large loss originated from company's decision in 1985 to engage in speculative investments (Zaitech) to try to offset a decrease in operating income that had occurred due to a sharp rise of the Japanese yen.
- In 1990, the bubble economy burst and Olympus incurred significant financial losses, which ballooned between 1997 and 1998.
- For many years Olympus kept the loss off of its own books by transferring financial assets that had declined in value to a series of companies that were not consolidated into Olympus's balance sheet. The loss was transferred by having these other entities (special-purpose entities) purchase the financial assets for their accounting book cost rather than their fair market value. The funds used by these other entities came from bank borrowing arranged by Olympus. Olympus therefore did not report any gain or loss on the sale.
- Management realized that it would be forced to disclose the financial losses due to the required change of accounting treatment, which would require consolidation of special-purpose entities and reporting of the assets at fair value in 2000.

- In essence, the scheme involved the company's placing collateral with foreign banks, who would then lend money to funds set up by Olympus to buy its own depressed assets at book value into special-purpose entities.
- Olympus engineered a plan to purchase these entities at a price much greater than their value (due to the embedded loss in those entities). Olympus recorded the excess of the purchase price over the fair value as goodwill. At the same time, Olympus overpaid for other acquisitions, apparently paying high "fees" that could be used to further obscure the losses. So, effectively, Olympus kept a liability and loss off of its books for many years (understating liabilities and overstating owners' equity) and when they repurchased the entity and were forced to record the liability, they overstated assets (goodwill) to compensate. This goodwill was then reported as being impaired over time to spread out the losses.
- To put the scale of the fraud in perspective, Olympus accumulated investment losses of ¥118 billion (US$1.5 billion) between 1990 until 2003; this compares to ¥1.7 billion (US$22 million) investment loss that the company reported for the financial year ended March 2000.
- ¥17 billion (US$218 million) was paid in expenses to brokers and bankers who helped to engineer these schemes. Key was the US$1.5 billion acquisition of U.K. medical technology maker Gyrus in February 2008, which included a US$687 million merger-and-acquisition fee, the highest in history.

Warning Signs

- Market commentators have cited the local Japanese corporate culture, which avoids conflict and up-front recognition of problems, as a key factor in allowing the fraud to have gone on for so long.
- Less than 3 percent of Japanese companies have audit committees. Most have a statutory auditor appointed by the president or CEO and approved by shareholders, and lack independent board directors.
- At Olympus, top management was dominated by strong personalities and had a culture that encouraged one-man decision making.
- Use of special-purpose entities that were initially not consolidated.
- Serial acquisitions with high prices and embedded fees with subsequent near-term write-offs of goodwill.

Key Lessons

- Losses can be hidden off balance sheet for many years.
- The auditors were also complicit in the scheme. In 2009, KPMG raised questions about Gyrus acquisition and qualified its approval of Gyrus accounts, but the Japanese affiliate chose not to reflect these concerns in the consolidated audit

OLYMPUS FINANCIAL DATA

USD m	Year ending March 30				
	2007	2008	2009	2010	2011
Balance Sheet					
Good will	668	3,009	1,867	2,097	2,111
i) of which goodwill associated with 3 acquired companies:	0	545	49	32	31
Calculated as:					
Book value at start of period	0	0	561	51	36
Increase	0	547	141	0	0
Write Off	0	(2)	(77)	(5)	(5)
Impairment	0	0	(575)	(14)	(0)
Book value at end of period	0	545	49	32	31
ii) of which goodwill associated with Gyrus acquisition:		1,689	1,365	1,728	1,627
Calculated as:					
Book value at start of period		1,497	1,740	1,426	1,924
Increase		0	2	0	0
Write Off / Impairment		0	(101)	(69)	(71)
Currency Exchange Adjustments		0	(148)	(73)	(131)
Fees Paid to Advisor		191	(128)	445	(95)
Book value at end of period		1,689	1,365	1,278	1,627
Cash flow					
Opreating Cashflow	920	893	430	824	396
Investing Cashflow	(819)	(3,054)	(214)	(227)	199
of which payments for Acquisitions	(20)	(2,331)	(1)	(4)	(148)
of which payments for additional stock investment in subs.	0	(184)	(418)	(647)	(70)
Free Cashflow Before Financing	101	(2,161)	216	597	595

Note: FX used to convert to USD based on agent rate on each relevant repeating date.

Sources: Company investigation report, company annual reports.

and shareholders were not informed. KPMG was replaced by Ernst & Young that year as the company's auditor.

- Poor corporate governance can enable accounting games to be played.

Case Study 3.3: Oceanus

Background

- Oceanus is a Singapore-listed food supplier specializing in the farming, processing, and sale of abalone and related products from its two farms in China.
- The company was listed on the Singapore Stock Exchange in 2008 through a reverse takeover of an existing public shell company.
- Oceanus reported strong top-line growth of 16.5 percent CAGR between 2008 and 2010, and the book value of its abalone assets grew from US$70 million to US$180 million over the same period.
- At the end of July 2011, the company had a listed market capitalization of US$310 million and an enterprise value of US$530 million.

What Happened

- The company issued a profit warning in August 2011, and in November 2011 reported a US$140 million write down of its abalone assets, resulting in a Q3 YTD net loss of US$103 million versus net profit of US$34 million over the same period last year.
- The write-down was due to an unexplained increase in mortality rates of its 200 million abalone population, resulting in 42 million abalones perishing versus 6 million reported over the same period in the previous year.
- Management attributed the loss to an operational misstep in growing larger abalones, and the CEO offered to resign pending an internal review.
- The share price had fallen more than 65 percent since the first profit warning, while cash reserves declined from US$15 million at the end of 2010 to US$4 million as of September 2011. As of March 2013 the company had little cash and negative working capital.

Warning Signs

- Despite reporting growing sales and large profits, actual sales of abalones had declined from 2008. The following information is extracted from Oceanus's 2010 annual report: actual sales of abalones were modest and declining while all of the profit could be attributed to gains in the value of abalones. The increase in value appeared to come primarily from an increase in the quantity of abalones (presumably from breeding) as opposed to the value per unit, which is peculiar given that the abalones should have also grown in size and value per unit. In its 2011 annual report, the company reported an RMB422 million loss from a decline in value related to price changes and an RMB367 million loss arising from mortality. At the end of 2011, the company reported total biological assets of RMB219 million and 134 million units, for a value per unit of 1.64 RMB. In hindsight, it appears that estimates of the quantity of abalones, their size/growth, and valuation in prior years may have been overstated.
- Large positive net profits were generated almost entirely from valuation gains of the abalone stock; adjusting for the gains resulted in significantly lower net profits.
- In 2010, a negative net profit was registered due to a large increase in expenses.
- Net cash flow and actual cash collection from abalone sales have been declining since 2008, while free cash flow (operating cash flow minus capital expenditures) has been consistently negative since listing.
- Oceanus has US$4 million of cash on the balance sheet as of Q3 2011, down from US$31 million at the end of Q3 2010 and US$88 million at the end of 2009.
- The founder and chairman, Dr. Ng Cher Yew, sits on the board of over 35 incorporated companies, and was a director of at least 3 companies that were dissolved or struck off the Companies' Register.

- Oceanus was listed via a reverse takeover, thereby avoiding the typical due diligence for a listing.

OCEANUS ANNUAL REPORT DATA

RMB Thousands	2010	2009	Change
Gain on biological assets	583,422	651,406	−10.44%
Sales of processed marine products	131,533	29,922	339.59%
Sales of food and beverage	71,341	36,306	96.50%
Total revenues	786,296	717,634	9.57%
Profit before income tax	232,827	412,318	−43.53%
Biological assets on balance sheet in thousands of RMB	1,154,580	831,000	38.94%
Purchases of biological assets in thousands of RMB	71,272	65,378	9.02%
Biological assets as a percentage of total assets	50.30%	38.80%	
Quantities of abalones (thousands of units)	178,358	119,775	48.91%
Value per unit RMB	6.47	6.94	−6.70%

Key Lessons

- Biological assets provide opportunities to report income that may not be realized in the future. Care must be taken in assessing the valuation of such assets. Footnotes must be scrutinized to look for discrepancies with what is going on relative to reported income and to the industry.
- It is difficult for boards of foreign-listed Chinese companies to monitor and control the onshore operating subsidiaries:
  - Both the Chairman and the auditors had limited access to information and limited cooperation from onshore employees.
  - Importance of legal representative and board control: Chairman was able to take control of the onshore subsidiary only after replacing the previous CEO. This had to be effected by the onshore entity's board, which, fortunately in this case, was controlled by the Singapore parent.
  - The new management team had to have physical possession of the company seal in order to take over daily operations.

NOTES

1. Note, however, that at the time of this writing, global standard setters were considering changing the standards to require putting an asset and corresponding liability on the balance sheet.
2. Current accounting standards are more restrictive in this regard than in the past. Many special-purpose entities must now be consolidated with the parent company's financial statements, rendering the game moot.
3. Note that some countries have yet to adopt IFRS, and individual country standards may not permit revaluation of assets.
4. Note that in subsequent years, if the fair value declines, the loss is offset against this holding account until it is used up before it is reported on the income statement.

REFERENCES

Muddy Waters Research. 2010. "Report of RINO International Corp.," October 11.
Oceanus Group. Annual Reports for 2010 and 2011.
Olympus Corporation, The Third Party Committee. 2011. "Investigation Report: Summary," December 6.
United States District Court for the District of Columbia. 2011. "*U.S. Securities and Exchange Commission v. Satyam Computer Services Limited d/b/a Mahindra Satyam,*" April 5.

CHAPTER 4

DETECTING EARNINGS MANAGEMENT

This chapter extends the material in the previous two chapters one step further, addressing multiyear manipulation. In a bid to smooth the volatility of earnings or manage the perceived trajectory of earnings, a company may purposefully understate earnings in the current year with the expectation of using this "cookie jar" reserve to boost earnings in later years. This chapter reveals the most common methods companies use to smooth variability and presents analysis techniques and warning signs to detect them.

Management may be incentivized to smooth the volatility or to alter the perceived trajectory of earnings. For example, a smooth earnings stream over time may be valued by creditors and investors, as it makes the company look more stable and less risky. However, creditors and investors would like to see smooth earnings only when it is real—when the underlying economics of the business are stable. If earnings is actually volatile but management engages in artificial means to make it appear smooth, then the true financial state of the company is not known to creditors and investors. Management may also have incentives to smooth out fluctuations if their compensation depends on it. For example, if management receives a lump-sum bonus only when earnings exceed a certain amount, management may be incentivized to "save" earnings in excess of the required to earn the bonus for a later year when earnings might be lower. Management may also want to alter the pattern of earnings to show a steady growth rate or other desired trajectory of earnings.

Recall from Chapter 1, when we presented our framework for evaluating financial statements, that the income statement is determined using the accrual basis of accounting. Revenue is reported when earned, not necessarily when the cash is received. Expenses are reported when incurred, not necessarily when paid. Further, some expenditures will not be considered "expenses" at the time they are incurred. For example, if the expenditure relates to the purchase of a capital asset, then it is reported as such on the balance sheet. The expense associated with this purchase will occur over time in the future as the asset depreciates in value. The accrual basis of accounting requires judgment, estimates, and assumptions. This creates the opportunity for management to make adjustments to the current period to increase (or decrease) earnings for that period. In previous chapters, we examined situations where a company was trying to increase earnings to a great extent or for a long period of time. Here, we examine situations where they may either increase or decrease earnings in one year, only to reverse this in a subsequent year. These adjustments may be subtle and often are not picked up in the press compared to more prominent irregularities that involve overstating earnings, financial positions, or cash flow.

ACCRUALS AND DEFERRALS REVISITED

As noted in earlier chapters, differences between the accrual-based income statement and the cash flow statement result in accruals and deferrals that are reflected on the balance sheet. Common accruals and deferrals are summarized in Exhibit 4.1. These accruals and deferrals can allow companies to move earnings from one period to the next or vice versa. This could create a smoother earnings trajectory in some cases or a more volatile one in other cases.

EXHIBIT 4.1   Common Accruals and Deferrals

	Revenue	Expense
Cash flows occur later than reflected in earnings	Asset	Liability
	Accounts Receivable	Accrued Expenses
		Deferred Tax Liability
		Contingencies
		Contra Asset
		Allowance for Doubtful Accounts
Cash flows occur before reflected in earnings	Liability	Asset
	Unearned Revenue	Property and Equipment
	Deferred Revenue	Prepaid Expense
		Deferred Tax Asset
		Deferred Expenses

ACCOUNTS RECEIVABLE (ACCRUED REVENUE) AND THE ALLOWANCE FOR DOUBTFUL ACCOUNTS

Accounts receivables arise when a company has made a sale and recorded the revenue on the income statement but has not yet collected the cash. This is permitted (even required) under the accrual basis of accounting. Accounting standards recognize, however, that some portion of accounts receivable may never be collected. The accrual basis of accounting requires that the company account for this possibility in order to match the expected bad debt expense with the same period in which the revenue is reported. Let's say that a company is new. It starts business in December 2013 and makes S$10 million of sales that month, none of which is collected. In the following year, a number of customers default on their obligations and the company collects only S$9.1 million. Absent the requirement to account for the potential bad debts at the time of the sale, the company would report S$10 million of 2013 revenues and a bad debt expense of S$0.9 million in 2014. This could be misleading—particularly if the company purposely had relaxed credit policies in order to maximize revenue in 2013. Accrual accounting requires that the company estimate in 2013 the amount of future noncollectible amounts to report an estimate of bad debt expense in 2013 rather than wait until the amount is known with certainty. Companies typically base this on their history of collectability relative to their credit standards. New companies can look to other companies in the same industry for initial estimates. These estimates may be based on a percentage of credit sales or a percentage of accounts receivable or based on an aging of accounts receivable (the longer the receivable has been outstanding, the higher the percentage).

Application: China Biotics

Extract from Form 10-K for FYE 31 March 2011

Allowance for doubtful accounts
We maintain an allowance for doubtful accounts for estimated losses that may result from the inability of our customers to make required payments. Such allowances are based upon several factors including, but not limited to, historical experience and the current and projected financial condition of specific customers. Since our inception of business, we have never experienced any unrecoverable receivables. We also have never experienced situations

(Continued)

(Continued)

causing us to cast doubt on the ability of our customers to make required payments. We had trade receivables totalling $26,194,313 and $21,008,664 as of March 31, 2011 and 2010, respectively, and no allowance for doubtful accounts for the years ended March 31, 2011 and 2010, respectively. We have considered all relevant factors, including the financial conditions, affecting the payment abilities of customers comprising these receivables up to the date of this 10-K, and we believe these customers are able to make required payments. We, however, cannot give assurance that these factors, including the financial conditions of these customers, will not change adversely in the future. We will continue to evaluate the ability of all our customers to make required payments. Were the financial condition of a customer to deteriorate, resulting in an impairment of its ability to make payments, allowances may be required.

While China Biotics acknowledged the requirement to set up an allowance for doubtful accounts, they chose not to, claiming that they have never had a situation where customers were not expected to make required payments. These claims are unlikely to play out positively over time and should be viewed with a great deal of scepticism.

For our preceding example, let's say that the company estimates, based on other companies in the same industry with similar credit policies, that 10 percent of its accounts receivable will be uncollectible. At the end of December 2013, it would report on its balance sheet:

Accounts Receivable—Gross	S$10,000,000
Less: Allowance for Doubtful Accounts	(1,000,000)
Accounts Receivable—Net	9,000,000

On the 2013 income statement, the company would report:

| Revenue | S$10,000,000 |
| Bad Debt Expense | 1,000,000 |

In 2014, the company discovers that the bad debts were only S$900,000. The company will not go back and change what was estimated in 2013, rather adjusting the allowance account for the current year (2014) and using the new information to create a refreshed 2014 estimate based on credit sales and receivables in that year.

Extending this example through 2014, assume that in 2014 the company had S$100 million credit sales. Collections during 2014 (including those related to 2013) were S$94.5 million. The company's accounts receivable balance at year-end 2014 would be:

Beginning balance	10,000,000
Actual bad debts	(900,000)
Credit sales	100,000,000
Collections	(94,500,000)
Ending balance	14,600,000

The company now estimates that its bad debts are expected to be 9 percent of the ending accounts receivable balance or S$1,314,000. The company's allowance account can be reconciled as follows:

Beginning balance	1,000,000
Actual bad debts	(900,000)
Bad debt expense for 2014	X
Ending balance	1,314,000

Bad debt expense for 2014 is determined based on what it would take to achieve the correct ending balance. It is therefore based on both the new estimate of bad debts for the current year plus an adjustment for difference between last period's estimates and actual bad debts. In this case, bad debt expense for 2014 would be S$1,214,000:

Beginning balance	1,000,000
Actual bad debts	(900,000)
Bad debt expense for 2014	1,214,000
Ending balance	1,314,000

Companies can manipulate their estimates to get desired results. Let's say in 2013 they wanted to boost earnings—they could have underestimated the bad debt expense in 2013. However, this would need to be reversed in the next year to catch up with the proper ending balance (or next year's estimate could also be underestimated to carry the problem to an even later year). Conversely, the company could have decided to overestimate bad debts in 2013 in order to "save up" some earnings for the following year.

Application: Harbin Electric

Harbin Electric is a Chinese company incorporated in Nevada and was publicly traded until taken private in 2011 after allegation of faulty accounting practices and a significant drop in its price per share. The following data were extracted from the company's U.S. Form 10-K filings (annual reports) for 2009 and 2010.

	Accounts Receivable	Allowance	Percentage Allowance
Year Ended 31 December 2008	30,437,235	153,155	0.5%
Year Ended 31 December 2009	97,302,153	3,979,268	4.1%
Year Ended 31 December 2010	93,392,999	7,493,667	8.0%
	Revenues	**A/R % of Rev**	**Allow. % of Rev**
Year Ended 31 December 2008	120,820,302	25.2%	0.1%
Year Ended 31 December 2009	223,234,394	43.6%	1.8%
Year Ended 31 December 2010	426,481,250	21.9%	1.8%
		Reported 2009	**Reported 2010**
Allowance for bad debts at 1 January 2008		116,238	
Recovery of bad debts		(1,899)	
Accounts receivable write off		—	
Increase in allowance from acquisition of Weihai		30,735	

	Reported 2009	Reported 2010
Effect of foreign currency translation	8,081	
Allowance for bad debts at 31 December 2008	**153,155**	**153,155**
Recovery of bad debts	(437,191)	(38,656)
Accounts receivable write-off	—	—
Effect of foreign currency translation		(24)
Increase in allowance from acquisition of Simo Motor	4,263,411	
Effect of foreign currency translation	(107)	
Allowance for bad debts at 31 December 2009	**3,979,268**	**114,475**
Increase in allowance		7,686,302
Negative provisions for allowance		(233,660)
Accounts receivable write off		—
Effect of foreign currency translation		(73,450)
Allowance for bad debts at 31 December 2009		**7,493,667**

In this case there are a number of oddities that should not occur in the normal course of business. First, the allowance account as a percentage of accounts receivable was relatively low in the first year and increased dramatically in the subsequent two years. It was also low in the first year relative to revenues but was exactly the same in the next two years as a percentage of sales. The pattern may indicate that the company is not accurately reflecting bad debts and may be understating the amount that will ultimately be collectible. The next oddity is that the company did not actually write off any bad debts in any of those years (see reconciliation of the allowance account) and in fact recorded "recoveries" of bad debts. The situation here should lead the analyst to question the legitimacy and collectability of the revenues and receivables.

DEFERRED (UNEARNED) REVENUE

While accounts receivables represent accrued revenue, revenue that is currently earned but not yet received, deferred revenue represents funds that have already been collected but are not yet reported as revenue. For example, a customer may make an advance payment (or deposit) for production of a custom-built machine. Until the machine is built and delivered to the customer, this advance payment must be accrued as a liability on the recipient's balance sheet. This liability will be settled either by delivery of the equipment or return of the amount deposited. In addition to the manufacture of custom products, similar advance payments may be required for the delivery of future services. The most common example is transportation where you purchase your airplane ticket or train ticket in advance of travel. While this is proper accounting treatment, it opens up the possibility that an unscrupulous manager will use it to smooth out income or otherwise move income from one period to another. If a manager wanted to move income to a later year, he could simply move current revenues into a liability account, asserting that current year collections relate to future deliveries. This account is typically titled "deferred revenue" or "unearned revenue." You should be skeptical of deferred or unearned revenue accounts for businesses where advance collection is not normal. For all companies, when you see these accounts, you should examine the balances from year to year to determine if their use increased or decreased revenue for the current year.

ACCRUED AND DEFERRED (PREPAID) EXPENSES

Accruals and deferrals occur for expenses as well. If a company has received goods or services but has not yet paid for them, then the amount owed must be accrued. In the case of goods, this accrual is called accounts payable. For other expenses, accrued expenses such as accrued wages, accrued taxes, accrued rent, and similar expense items are set up as liabilities. Companies can over- or underestimate these accruals to move expenses (and hence income) from one year to another. The existence of accrued expenses and accounts payable is common for all companies, so their existence alone should not cause concern. You should be concerned when the level or change in these items has a significant impact on earnings for the current period.

The opposite of an accrued expense is a deferred expense. A simple example occurs when a company makes a payment in advance related to a future expense. For example, let's say that a company pays its rent for a two-year period in advance. The expense will be reported over the next two years, so the payment is initially recorded as an asset, prepaid rent, rather than an expense. Over the next two years, it will move the balance out of the prepaid rent account on the balance sheet and report it as an expense on the income statement. Common examples of deferred or prepaid expenses are rent, insurance, and similar items that are utilized over an extended tenure.

Deferred expenses also occur for major items such as the purchase of property, plant, and equipment. The equipment is not expensed immediately. Instead it is capitalized as an asset and expensed over time. As we noted in Chapter 2, companies can misclassify an expense as a purchase of property and equipment or an intangible asset, resulting in an asset on the balance sheet rather than a current expense. This creates a type of deferred asset, although it may not have *deferred* in its name. Other companies have created special categories on their balance sheet for these deferred expenses such as "deferred customer acquisition costs." Sometimes these may be legitimate, such as in the insurance industry, but other times it is simply a way to avoid reporting marketing expenses on the income statement currently. Deferred assets of any type on a balance sheet should be examined to make sure they make sense given the company's business model, but nevertheless should always be viewed skeptically.

DEFERRED TAXES

Deferred taxes represent a special case and can result in either a deferred asset or a deferred liability. They arise from differences in how items of revenue and expense are reported on financial statements depending on whether they are being prepared for investors or on tax returns prepared for government agencies. Sometimes these are the same, but more likely the government's rules differ from accounting standards for reporting to public investors.

Let's first look at a common situation to see how deferred taxes can arise (see Exhibit 4.2). AP Apparel, Inc. (APAI) purchased $500,000 worth of equipment during 2013 for use in its manufacturing operations. APAI had recently been incorporated upon issuance of $600,000 of common stock. APAI's balance sheet immediately after the purchase is shown in Exhibit 4.2.

EXHIBIT 4.2   APAI, Inc. Balance Sheet July 2013

Cash	$100,000
Property, plant, and equipment	$500,000
Total assets	$600,000
Common stock	$600,000
Total liabilities and equity	$600,000

For accounting, APAI will depreciate the equipment on a straight-line basis over five years with no salvage value. Because it acquired the equipment during the year, in 2013 it will take half the annual depreciation amount (referred to as the half-year convention). The depreciation each year is as follows:

Year	"Book" Depreciation Expense	Accumulated Depreciation
2013	$ 50,000	$ 50,000
2014	$100,000	$150,000
2015	$100,000	$250,000
2016	$100,000	$350,000
2017	$100,000	$450,000
2018	$ 50,000	$500,000

For tax purposes, APAI's country of operations requires that equipment be depreciated on a specific schedule where depreciation is accelerated:

Year	Rate	"Tax" Depreciation Expense	Accumulated Deprecation
2013	20.00%	$100,000	$100,000
2014	32.00%	$160,000	$260,000
2015	19.20%	$ 96,000	$356,000
2016	11.52%	$ 57,600	$413,600
2017	11.52%	$ 57,600	$471,200
2018	5.76%	$ 28,800	$500,000

APAI expects to generate revenues of $250,000 per year with cash operating expenses of $100,000, excluding taxes and depreciation. Assume that the company invests the net cash amount at the end of each year to earn a 6 percent return in the subsequent year. Further assume that the tax rate currently applied is 30 percent for all periods. APAI's expected taxable income, tax payments, and cash flow for each year are shown in Exhibit 4.3. For the six-year period, APAI has cumulative taxable income of $563,203 and cumulative taxes due of $168,962 for an after-tax income of $394,241.

Exhibit 4.4 shows the income to be reported for "book" purposes. The cumulative pretax income, net income, and cash flow are the same as the tax reporting

EXHIBIT 4.3   APAI Taxable Income and Taxes Payable

	2013	2014	2015	2016	2017	2018	Total
Revenues	250,000	250,000	250,000	250,000	250,000	250,000	1,500,000
Interest income	0	14,100	23,872	32,903	41,622	50,706	163,203
Cash expenses	(100,000)	(100,000)	(100,000)	(100,000)	(100,000)	(100,000)	(600,000)
Depreciation	(100,000)	(160,000)	(96,000)	(57,600)	(57,600)	(28,800)	(500,000)
Taxable income	50,000	4,100	77,872	125,303	134,022	171,906	563,203
Taxes payable	15,000	1,230	23,362	37,591	40,207	51,572	168,962

EXHIBIT 4.4   APAI Reported Financial Statements

Year	2013	2014	2015	2016	2017	2018	Total
Revenues	250,000	250,000	250,000	250,000	250,000	250,000	1,500,000
Cash expenses	(100,000)	(100,000)	(100,000)	(100,000)	(100,000)	(100,000)	(600,000)
Depreciation	(50,000)	(100,000)	(100,000)	(100,000)	(100,000)	(50,000)	(500,000)
Operating income	100,000	50,000	50,000	50,000	50,000	100,000	400,000
Interest income	0	14,100	23,872	32,903	41,622	50,706	163,203
Pretax income	100,000	64,100	73,872	82,903	91,622	150,706	563,203
Tax expense	30,000	19,230	22,162	24,871	27,487	45,212	168,962
Net income	70,000	44,870	51,710	58,032	64,135	105,494	394,241

numbers. However, there is a difference in the timing of the reported income. For 2013, reported pretax income is $100,000 for "book" purposes versus $50,000 for tax purposes. While the actual taxes paid for 2013 are $15,000, the income statement provides for $30,000 in tax expense. It would not be appropriate to show only the $15,000 paid as tax expense for income statement purposes since this would give a financial statement user the impression that the effective tax rate was only 15 percent ($15,000/$100,000). In order to provide a proper matching of tax expense with the related income, tax expense is reported as the amount expected to be paid on $100,000 of pretax financial income. This is 30 percent of 100,000, or $30,000. This $15,000 difference between the tax expense ($30,000) and the taxes paid ($15,000) for 2013 is a deferred tax. In this case, APAI will have to pay the additional taxes in subsequent periods. This results in a deferred tax liability.

The total tax expense for 2013 can be broken down as follows:

Current tax expense	$15,000
Deferred tax expense	15,000
Total tax expense	$30,000

The balance sheet at the end of 2013 would appear as follows:

APAI, INC. BALANCE SHEET, YEAR-END 2013

Cash	$235,000
Property, plant and equipment (net)	450,000
Total assets	$685,000
Deferred tax liability	$ 15,000
Common stock	600,000
Retained earnings	70,000
Total liabilities and equity	$685,000

When is this deferred tax liability "due"? We need to look at when the temporary difference is expected to reverse. The tax expense for investor reporting and tax purposes by year are:

Year	GAAP	Tax	Current Year Difference	Cumulative Difference
2013	$30,000	$15,000	$15,000	$15,000
2014	19,230	1,230	18,000	33,000
2015	22,162	23,362	(1,200)	31,800
2016	24,871	37,591	(12,720)	19,080
2017	27,487	40,207	(12,720)	6,360
2018	45,212	51,572	(6,360)	0
Total	168,962	168,962		

So the initial deferred tax liability is created in 2013 and increased in 2014. The liability begins to decline in 2015 as the temporary difference reverses. At the end of the six-year period, the deferred tax liability returns to zero. This is a common situation, and you should expect to see deferred tax liabilities on a company's financial statements.

Deferred tax assets are less common as they arise when a company reports higher income for tax purposes than investor reporting purposes (the opposite of the preceding scenario). The most common deferred tax asset occurs when the company has a loss for accounting purposes that cannot currently be deducted for tax purposes but can be carried forward to offset taxable income in later years.

Let's say that in the first year of business a company has a pretax loss of HKD 1 million and that tax rules permit it to carry this loss over to offset profits in later years. Assuming a 15 percent tax rate, the company would report net loss of HKD 850,000 (HKD 1 million of pretax loss offset by a negative tax expense of HKD 150,000). This would result in a deferred tax asset of HKD 150,000 since no tax refund is currently received—the company is hopeful that it will be profitable in future years and be able to reduce taxes by that amount. If a company is doubtful that it will realize the full benefit, it is required to set up a valuation allowance to reduce the deferred tax asset and net income in the current year. For example, if it feels that only half of the carryforward will be utilized, it would reduce the deferred tax asset to HKD 75,000 and report a loss of HKD 925,000. Since this involves management's discretion, it is another area where management can manipulate the amount of earnings reported in a particular year by moving expenses or income from one year to another.

If a company has deferred tax liabilities or assets, you should examine the footnotes to make sure the reasons for their existence makes sense. You should be particularly skeptical about deferred tax assets and watch carefully for companies where the related valuation allowance fluctuates dramatically from year to year.

Application: West China Cement

The following table presents income tax expense for West China Cement from 2009 to 2012 (thousands of RMB).

	2012	2011	2010	2009
Current Tax	74,245	112,972	57,429	—
Deferred Tax	11,813	(10,084)	(12,742)	11,566
Income Tax Expense	86,058	102,888	44,687	11,566

In some years income tax expense is increased while in other years decreased due to deferred taxes and other similar amounts. The footnotes to the financial statements reveal that most of the changes come from deferred tax assets and that as of FYE 2012, the company had deferred tax assets of 36.755 in thousands of RMB resulting from losses carried forward. It is quite possible that these deferred tax assets may need to be written down in value if their use is disallowed.

CONTINGENCIES AND RESERVES

Companies can make other adjustments to net income over multiple periods by setting up contingent losses or so-called reserves ("cookie jar reserves" where they can dip into the cookie jar as needed in future years) using a variety of accounting techniques. For example, companies are required to accrue contingent liabilities if they are probable and can be reasonably estimated. Let's say a company is having a particularly good year and would like to "save" some of the income for a future year. The company can overstate a contingent loss (or create a new one), reducing income in the current year and setting up a liability for the potential loss. In a later year, when the loss is settled or deemed to no longer exist, the liability is reduced and a gain is reported on the income statement for the "recovery or increase in value." A variety of terminologies may be used. Look out and scrutinize disclosures of contingent losses/liabilities, reserves, derivative liabilities, and similar terminology.

Application: China Biotics

Footnote disclosure from 10-K FYE 31 March 2011, regarding a $25 million note issued in 2007 and due in December 2010:

> The note was secured by a pledge of 100% of the stock of SGI. In addition, Mr. Song Jinan, the Company's Chief Executive Officer and largest shareholder, agreed to guarantee the Company's obligations under the Note with a pledge of 4,000,000 shares of the Company's common stock owned by Mr. Song. The note was convertible at an exercise price of $12 per share into shares of the Company's common stock at any time until maturity. If the Note was not converted before maturity, the Company agreed to redeem the Note with a total yield of 10% per annum. The Note also included a mandatory conversion into the Company's common stock if the Company achieved net income of $60 million in fiscal year 2010. For the year ended March 31, 2010, the Company had net income of $15.6 million.

Clearly, the net income for the fiscal year ended 31 March 2010, was a significant number. If it were too high, it could have triggered the convertible feature of this note and diluted the ownership of the CEO. Interestingly, the company used the note itself to reduce income in 2010. The company determined that there was a derivative liability embedded in this note in 2010 (but not prior years) and set up a liability of over $12 million, reducing net income in that year by $12 million (without this liability net income would still have been lower than $60 million but certainly made the difference from $60 million larger). In the following year, after the note matured and was paid off, it eliminated the liability and reported a $12 million gain.

PARTING COMMENTS

The accounting games demonstrated in this chapter can be quite subtle. Often, they are found together where a company uses all of the devices available to manage the volatility of earnings. Detection of these games requires scrutiny of the footnotes to determine the level of accruals and deferrals relative to reported net income. Exhibit 4.5 summarizes warning signs to be on the lookout for to detect earnings manipulation.

EXHIBIT 4.5   Checklist of Warning Signs and Analysis Techniques for Earnings Management

Allowance for Doubtful Accounts	• Examine the allowance for doubtful accounts and bad debt expense relative to accounts receivable and revenue over time. Look for irregular patterns. • Examine the level of actual bad debts over time relative to the company's estimate in prior years.
Deferred or Unearned Income	• Look for accounts labeled deferred revenue or unearned revenue. • Consider whether advance collection is normal for this type of business. Does the deferral make sense? • Examine the balances from year to year to determine if their use increased or decreased revenue for the current year. • What would the company's revenue and profit have looked like without this deferral? Does it look like the company is purposefully saving income for a later year?
Accrued and Deferred Expenses	• Are there significant accrued expenses relative to net income, and do they fluctuate by large amounts? • Are there any deferred expenses listed as an asset on the balance sheet (other than deferred taxes)? • Are there any unusual assets or unexplained large increases in assets, particularly relative to the increase in revenues?
Deferred Taxes	• Does the company's net deferred tax impact on net income fluctuate from a positive to a negative impact? • Does the company have significant deferred tax assets? Is it plausible that they will be usable in subsequent years? • Did the company establish a valuation allowance for deferred tax assets, and has it fluctuated in value over time?

Contingencies and Reserves	• Scrutinize disclosures both on the balance sheet and footnotes for:
	  • Contingent losses
	  • Contingent liabilities
	  • Reserves
	  • Derivative liabilities
	  • Similar terminology
	• Consider whether the company appears to be creating a cookie jar reserve.

CASE STUDIES

The following cases examine companies that may have been accused—but not necessarily ascertained guilty—of manipulating their reported results. These cases demonstrate many of the concepts presented in this chapter. Note that some concepts in these cases may be related to concepts covered in other chapters; however the full case is included for completeness and to demonstrate that there is often a plural nature of accounting manipulation.

Case Study 4.1: Harbin Electric (Nasdaq: HRBN)

Background

- Harbin Electric is a holding company incorporated in Nevada, with its principal place of business based in Harbin, China. As of its last traded price at $23.30, it had a market cap of US$434.58 million. The company became a public company in the United States in 2005 after completing a reverse merger with public shell company Torch.
- Through its U.S.- and China-based subsidiaries, the company designs, develops, manufactures, supplies, and services a wide range of electric motors. Products are mainly sold in China, but also internationally in North America, and to a lesser degree in Southeast Asia and Africa. HRBN is based in Harbin, China, along with its wholly owned subsidiaries.
- HRBN targets its products to the global original equipment manufacturers as components or in integrated systems, and cooperates with major system integrators to jointly develop and market new products.
- The company's suppliers include GuiYang Putian Wanxiang Logistic Technology, Daqing Oil Field, Suifenghe Wanrong Business Trade, and Shanghai Junci Machine and Electric Equipments Co. Ltd.
- The company offers three product lines: (1) linear motors and their integrated application systems, (2) automobile specialty micromotors, and (3) industrial rotary motors. HRBN operates three manufacturing facilities in China, which are wholly owned subsidiaries.
- HRBN operated through its indirect wholly owned subsidiaries: Harbin Tech Full Electric Co. Ltd. (HTFE) and Weihai Hengda Electric Motor Co. Ltd. (Hengda). On 10 July 2008, HTFE acquired Hengda, by paying approximately US$54 million (RMB370 million) in cash in 2008 and the remaining balance of US$0.7 million (RMB5 million) within two years from the agreement. The transaction was closed on 15 July 2008. In October 2008, the company, through another indirect wholly owned subsidiary, Advanced Automation Group, LLC (AAG), formed Advanced Automation Group Shanghai Co. Ltd. (AAG Shanghai), to design, develop, manufacture, sell, and service custom industrial automation controllers for linear motors.
- At first glance, HRBN's revenues easily beat estimates and the competition from 2008 to 2010. Reported revenues saw an increase of +86 percent from 2008 to 2009 (US$120 million to US$223.2 million), and +91 percent from 2000–2010 (US$223.2 million to US$426.5 million), with gross profits increasing from US$47.48 million in 2008 by a whopping 300 percent to US$135.7 million in 2010. Operating income grew 47.6 percent from 2008 to 2009, and 50.2 percent from 2009 to 2010. The company appeared to be growing very rapidly, with profitability from operations higher than the competition. Despite the strong growth, dividends were not paid out as the company stated it was growing significantly and had better use of the cash for expansion plans.

- However, on closer inspection, the company had negative free cash flows despite great revenue growth. In 2008 to 2010, *cash flow used in investing* exceeded *cash provided by operations* in the range of 92.8 percent in 2008 (–US$81.1 million vs. +US$42.3 million) to 19.5 percent in 2010 (–US$111.5 million vs. +US$93.3 million).

	2010	2009	2008
Revenues	**$426,481,250**	**$223,234,394**	**$120,820,302**
Cost of Sales	290,768,312	146,622,220	73,343,521
Gross Profit	135,712,938	76,612,174	47,476,781
Research and Development Expense	3,423,386	2,093,366	1,170,169
Selling, General and Administrative Expenses	38,974,147	18,671,507	11,913,435
Income from Operations	**93,315,405**	**55,847,301**	**34,393,177**
Other Expense (Income), Net			
Other Income, Net	(5,489,629)	(5,462,148)	(1,575,224)
Interest Expense, Net	4,593,099	12,315,645	6,065,814
Loss on Currency Hedge Settlement	—	9,000,000	—
Gain on Debt Repurchase	—	(4,155,000)	—
Loss from Disposal of Subdivision	623,158	—	—
Change in Fair Value of Warrants	(574,131)	13,214,525	—
Total Other (Income) Expense, Net	(847,503)	24,913,022	4,490,590
Income before Provision for Income Taxes	94,162,908	30,934,279	29,902,587
Provision for Income Taxes	14,915,151	7,796,084	4,523,888
Net Income before Noncontrolling Interest	79,247,757	23,138,195	25,378,699
Comprehensive Income	$90,514,002	$16,340,411	$39,974,020

	2010 (Restated)	2009 (Restated)	2008
Cash Flows from Operating Activities:			
Net Income Attributable to Noncontrolling Interest	$2,432,411	$3,491,414	$—
Net Income Attributable to Controlling Interest	76,815,346	19,646,781	25,378,699
Consolidated Net Income	79,247,757	23,138,195	25,378,699
Adjustments to Reconcile Net Income to Cash			
Provided by (Used in) Operating Activities:			
Net Cash Provided by Operating Activities	**93,282,848**	**62,516,753**	**42,305,045**
Cash Flows from Investing Activities			
Purchase of Plant and Equipment	(19,510,180)	(8,478,159)	(16,035,159)
Proceeds from Disposal of Plant and Equipment	206,509	282,877	—
Additions to Construction-in-Progress	(1,010,284)	(3,733,692)	(16,386,519)
Payment to Original Shareholders for Acquisition	**(27,230,236)**	(83,958,460)	(53,335,500)
Payment to Acquire Noncontrolling Interests	**(27,684,220)**	—	—
Deconsolidation of Cash Held in Disposed Subdivisions	(602,948)	—	—
Proceeds from Sale of Controlling Interests in Subsidiaries	1,846,105	—	—
Net Cash Used in Investing Activities	**(111,457,700)**	**(89,122,339)**	**(81,099,041)**

- "Payment to Acquire Noncontrolling Interests" of US$27.68 million was for one of HRBN's subsidiaries, Simo Motor. Citron Research stated that Simo Motor had issues with its cash reconciliation, accounts payables/receivables, and inventory valuation. The main physical plant of Simo Motor was a 50-year-old facility, with lack of automation in its manufacturing, requiring capex for retooling in order to remain competitive. However, in HRBN's FY2010 annual report, the company stated goodwill of US$41.8 million for the acquisition of Simo Motor for its proprietary manufacturing process, despite its outdatedness.
- "Payment to Original Shareholders for Acquisition" of US$27.23 million was due to original shareholders that were unpaid for the acquisition of Simo Motor and Weihai in 2009 and 2010. The subsidiaries' shareholders were not mentioned in HRBN's FY2010 annual report.
- Ownership and capital structure:
  - Major shareholders:
    - Tianfu Yang: 40.7 percent
    - Orchard Capital: 6.3 percent
    - Abax: 5.4 percent
  - In 2004, CEO Yang and his brother Tianli Yang, fraudulently obtained the official seal of China Construction Import Export Corp (CCIE) to guarantee a loan for HRBN. In the settlement agreement with CCIE, Tianfu Yang admitted guilt in order to get CCIE to agree to drop criminal proceedings in the matter. Of the subsidiaries of HRBN, CEO Tianfu Yang owned 100 percent of Harbin Tech Full Electric.

Subsidiaries of Harbin Electric	Place Incorporated	Ownership
Advanced Electric Motors, Inc. (AEM)	Delaware, USA	100%
Harbin Tech Full Electric Co. Ltd. (HTFE)	**Harbin, China**	**100%**
Advanced Automation Group, LLC (AAG)	Delaware, USA	51%
Advanced Automation Group Shanghai Co. Ltd. (SAAG)	Shanghai, China	51%
Shanghai Tech Full Electric Co. Ltd. (STFE)	Shanghai, China	100%
Weihai Tech Full Simo Motor Co. Ltd. (Weihai)	Weihai, China	100%
Xi'an Tech Full Simo Motor Co. Ltd. (Simo Motor)	Xi'an, China	100%

Source: 10-K Annual Report FY2010 from SEC website.

- Background on board of directors:
  - *Boyd Plowman* is head of the audit committee of HRBN, and appointed head of special committee to take HRBN private. He was also serving as a director of several Abax-controlled entities, including Abax Global Opportunities Fund, Abax Arhat Fund, Abax Claremont Ltd., Abax Jade Ltd., Abax Emerald Ltd., Abax Lotus Ltd., Abax Nai Xin A Ltd., and Abax Nai Xin B Ltd. (the Abax Companies). Plowman was sued by the trustee of his former employer, who is now in bankruptcy.
  - *David Gatton* was a member of the board of directors of Bodisen Biotech, one of the first and most notorious of the Chinese frauds. In November 2011, he resigned as Harbin's director.
  - *Zedong Xu (CFO)* was chief financial officer (CFO) of HRBN from 2003 to November 2011. From September 1998 to 2000, he was the CFO for Harbin WanDa Electrical home appliances. From 1996 to 1998, he was a financial manager for Harbin High Technology Torch Daya Real Estate Co. Ltd.

What Happened?

- On 11 October 2010, the Harbin board announced that it had received a non-binding proposal from its CEO and chairman, Tianfu Yang, and Baring Private Equity Asia Group Ltd. to take the company private, at $24/share, 36 percent higher than its 20-day trading average. Goldman Sachs was to serve as financial adviser to Yang. Analysts at Maxim Group, LLC and Roth Capital Partners, LLC, two firms that covered HRBN, rated the stock a "buy" with a target of $24, equal to the offer price. Maxim's analyst stated that Harbin Electric's financial statements were "most likely" reliable.
- However, in November 2010, HRBN put out a press release stating that Baring's participation in the deal would be limited to a right, not an obligation, to provide up to 10 percent of equity and/or debt financing, stating that HRBN's intention was to pursue the $24/share private buyout offer and seek alternative sources of financing. At that time, HRBN's shares were trading at US$16.45 in the premarket.
- In the same month, CEO Yang entered into a term loan facility with China Development Bank (CDB) for US$50 million, of which $15 million was earmarked to pay off outstanding short-term debt. CDB did not securitize the loan with assets of HRBN or with its cash flow, but instead collateralized the loan with 7 million shares of Harbin stock pledged by the CEO, with provisions calling for him to pledge additional shares if the price went lower. At the time of transaction, the 7 million shares were worth US$140 million collateral value for a $50 million loan.

- A special committee in HRBN was set up to look into the privatization process and to aid CEO Yang in finding a suitable buyer for the company. In the seven months (November 2010 to May 2011) leading up to the privatization, there was no announcement from CEO Yang about an official buyout, or the decision process to which the special committee was adhering. The market's scepticism of the deal completing was reflected in HRBN's 31 percent decline since CEO Yang first disclosed his intention in November 2010. Over the period from November 2010 to June 2011, the amount of short selling increased to 4.7 million shares, representing a record 28 percent of shares available for trading.
- Then, in April 2011, HRBN announced that the CDB was committing US$400 million term loan facility, coupled with Abax's contributing financing of up to US$63.8 million for the private buyout. Abax was a US$900 million fund backed by Morgan Stanley, coupled with the CDB as anchor investor. According to a May 2011 regulatory filing, the costs to take HRBN private was US$463.8 million, at $24/share. This arrangement with the CDB and Abax gave CEO Yang the required funds. Morgan Stanley was also the financial adviser to HRBN's special committee for the deal.
- On 7 June 2011, Harbin Electric fell 5.9 percent to US$13.68, leaving the stock $10.32 below Yang's $24/share offer. The 75 percent difference was the widest of any all-cash offer of more than US$500 million globally.
- In May 2011, HRBN received calls and e-mails from a number of investment professionals asking about rumors that CEO Yang and CFO Zedong Xu had gone missing. HRBN's share price plummeted to below $6 from $15 before rebounding to around $8 by the end of the week. In a later statement, HRBN and its management categorically denied the rumors and reported that the entire management team including CEO Yang and CFO Xu were at work, performing their respective corporate duties.
- In June 2011, Harbin Electric signed an agreement to be sold for $24 per share to HTFE, which was controlled by CEO Tianfu Yang. The deal valued HRBN at US$750 million. Following the announcement of the management-led buyout, HRBN's stock jumped to $13. It was still significantly below the proposed takeover price of $24/share, suggesting investor confidence remained rattled. At its last traded price, it had a market capitalization of US$442.82 million.
- On 3 November 2011, HRBN announced the completion of the merger contemplated by the Agreement and Plan of Merger, dated 19 Jun 2011. The company became a wholly owned subsidiary of Tech Full Electric Company Limited, controlled by HRBN's CEO Yang.

Warning Signs

- *Mismatch between China's State Administration of Industry & Commerce (SAIC) and SEC's filings.* Consolidation of HRBN's four subsidiaries based on subsidiaries' Chinese filings in SAIC showed approximately US$12 million versus US$80 million net income reported on its SEC filings in 2010.

In addition, HRBN understated its liabilities on its SEC filings versus a consolidated version including all of its subsidiaries under SAIC filings. In 2010, HRBN showed total liability of US$180 million on its SEC filings versus consolidation of subsidiaries of US$244 million in SAIC.

SAIC filings revealed low profitability and undisclosed liabilities from its subsidiaries: HTFE reported losses of US$1 million in FY2009 and US$3 million in 2010, in addition to subsidiary STFE's reporting losses of US$2 million and US$1.3 million, respectively.

- *Off-the-charts financial results without independent verification.* HRBN doubled revenue in 2009 and 2010, to a run rate of greater than US$500 million per year, and showed net margins besting peer competitors. Yet it did not disclose a single verifiable large customer or a large-scale order with a verifiable counterparty. Its major customers from prior years' filings stated little or no business conducted with Harbin. HRBN's most recent operating margin of about 20 percent was three times higher than its mainland China peers.

- *HRBN's auditor, Frazer Frost, is a firm that no longer exists,* as Frazer and Frost have dissolved their partnership due to SEC sanctions for shoddy work practices and failure to detect fraud at RINO International, another Chinese company. Frazer nevertheless remains HRBN's auditor. The stigma of HRBN's not using one of the Big Four auditors raises questions about their internal numbers, even despite their use of "white shoe" bankers Goldman Sachs and Morgan Stanley.

- *High revenue growth, but an absence of verifiable customers.* The linear and micromotor division creates custom motor solutions, and therefore HRBN should have a portfolio of customers with large-scale production orders. HRBN's revenue growth claims were huge: it stated it was doing more business in 2Q2011 than it did in FY2008—a 400 percent increase in just over two years—and at very high margins. But not a single customer of significant size can be independently confirmed. With a US$500 million/year run rate, there are no customers with verifiable revenue of more than US$10 million/year. Harbin stopped disclosing customer concentration identities and percentages in 2010. HRBN's largest customer in 2008 (number 2 in 2009), Jiangsu Liyang Car Seat Adjuster, does not manufacture or sell electric seat adjusters (after a brief attempt to expand into that product line) and states that it buys no electric motors. HRBN was also not willing to disclose or discuss customers even with a possible suitor, who was brought to the table by Morgan Stanley.

- *Land transactions that do not match.* In June 2011, HRBN abruptly announced that it was putting down a US$23 million (RMB$150 million) cash deposit on land rights for a new factory in Xi'an Lintong, China. The term of the Simo Land Use Agreement was 50 years, and the aggregate amount that Simo Motor would

	Revenues		
Product Line	2010	2009	2008
Linear Motors and Related Systems	$76,334,053	$60,640,554	$49,785,537
Specialty Micro-Motors	60,766,922	40,231,091	34,195,658
Rotary Motors			
Weihai	93,249,223	72,240,555	27,609,487
Xi'an	188,464,807	44,068,683	—
Others	7,666,245	6,053,511	9,229,620
Total	$426,481,250	$223,234,394	$120,820,302

	Cost of Sales		
Product Line	2010	2009	2008
Linear Motors and Related Systems	$30,400,634	$24,684,185	$23,035,347
Specialty Micro-Motors	39,964,248	24,451,557	20,605,970
Rotary Motors			
Weihai	82,440,427	64,182,822	24,578,224
Xi'an	133,137,128	30,128,005	—
Others	4,825,875	3,175,651	5,123,980
Total	$290,768,312	$146,622,220	$73,343,521

Source: 10-K Annual Report FY2010 from SEC website.

pay was approximately US$38.8 million (RMB$250 million) for 500 Mu of industrial land. This transaction was never disclosed in a press release, nor was it disclosed in a conference call or investor presentation. It appeared only in a filing in 1Q11's 10-Q. The coincidence was that the purchase price was almost exactly HRBN's pretax net income reported for 1Q11 of U.S. dollars.

The price HRBN paid for the most recent land transaction worked out to be RMB$500,000 per Mu, suggesting serious inflation compared to corresponding land bureau records. Bureau records in 2008 showed that a purchase of 242.85 Mu of land in the exact same industrial park worked out to

RMB$70,000 per Mu—a 700 percent appreciation in three years, which is not credible.

- *Unnecessary cash-up-front "fees" to undisclosed parties.* In February 2011, HRBN entered into a consulting service agreement with a third party, which agreed to provide advisory and consulting services to obtain financing in the Chinese capital markets for a period of five years from 2011 to 2015. The service fee was nonrefundable and amounted to US$3 million, of which HRBN paid US$2.9 million up front.

- *Lack of transparency.* HRBN's special committee did not provide up-to-date news of their decision-making process. U.S. investors' expectation of much higher levels of disclosure and trustworthiness of information released by companies, and the overhang of the SEC's announcement in 2010 of its intention to investigate the use of reverse takeovers, caused investors to sell down the stock. The only missing piece was a *signed definitive merger agreement* from the special committee. The process the special committee instituted seemed irregular, though the relative lack of transparency is not basis enough to warrant a declaration of fraud.

Key Lessons

- HRBN's private buyout proposal garnered attention for being the first of its kind involving a U.S.-traded Chinese stock. Part of the problem was the constant accounting scandals and earnings restatements (and fraud) that dogged Chinese stocks, which resulted in a major risk discounting in shares. While many Chinese stocks deserve this toxic reputation, HRBN was not confirmed to be a fraudulent company.

- The loss of trust in Chinese companies such as Rino (Muddy Waters Research: Rino overstated sales and claimed contracts that didn't exist) and China MediaExpress (Citron Research: China MediaExpress's auditor, Deloitte, quit after stating it lost confidence in the representations of management) gave the view that HRBN was in the same category as these firms—fraudulent accounting by Chinese companies.

- The lack of transparency from the special committee, choice of a relatively boutique auditor, negative cash flows despite great revenue growth, coupled with up-front payment fees for consultation and huge land price transactions, resulted in the perception that management was engaged in misrepresentation and fraudulent activities.

- However, CEO Yang seemed serious about taking HRBN private and was able to keep his shareholders happy with the US$24 per share buyout. Management had noted on numerous occasions its valuation was unwarrantedly poor due to the significant amount of false and misleading information introduced into the market (i.e., Citron Research), though he reiterated at the end of the day that he had the shareholders' interests at heart.

- It remains to be seen if the SEC and/or the SAIC would take action to look through the accounting books of Harbin Electric, given that the majority of HRBN's shareholders have been happy with the buyout offer.

Case Study 4.2: West China Cement

Background

- West China Cement (WCC) is a cement manufacturer in China operating primarily in the Shaanxi province. It has a total of 17 production lines, with a total capacity of approximately 23 million tons per annum.
- WCC was listed on the LSE Alternative Investment Market in 2006, before delisting in August 2010 and listing on the HK Exchange. It had a market cap of US$762.2 million as of 10 August 2012.

Key Financials (US$ million)	
Market cap	763
Net debt	441.3
LTM revenue	506.1
LTM EBITDA	181
LTM net profit	105
Total debt/EBITDA	2.9×
Net debt/EBITDA	2.4×
EV/EBITDA	6.7×
P/E	6.7×
P/B	1.1×

What Happened

- On 12 July 2011, Moody's Investors Service released a report identifying red flags in the corporate governance of certain companies in China. WCC, along with four other companies, was identified as having the most red flags. WCC's share price fell by 14.4 percent.

- On 8 August 2012, Glaucus Research issued a Strong Sell recommendation on WCC, calling it a "blatant fraud." WCC's share price fell initially by only 1.5 percent. Glaucus's major points were:
  - WCC's margins are fabricated. Despite selling a commodity in a hypercompetitive market, its margins are 20 percentage points higher than its H-share, A-share, and local competitors.
  - WCC appears to be massively overpaying for loss-making cement factories.
  - WCC pursues expensive financing despite generating healthy free cash flow from operations.
  - WCC has had abnormally high auditor and management turnover.
  - WCC's corporate governance figureheads have been tainted by past scandals.
- WCC's management issued a point-by-point response the following day and flew to Hong Kong for an investor presentation.
- In March 2013, the company announced plans to slow production of cement in spite of high demand to focus on reducing debt, which would indicate that growth in revenues may not be profitable.
- As of October 2013, the market capitalization of the company had fallen about 15 percent; however, the company continues to operate and there has been no further news on the allegations.

WCC/Deutsche Bank's response:

- WCC's prices are lower because it reports prices at ex-factory prices, which do not include transportation costs, whereas the prices obtained by Glaucus from Digital Cement are based on actual transacted prices.
- Market prices reported by Digital Cement represent prices only in Xi'an (the capital of Shaanxi) and not throughout Shaanxi. In general, there is a disparity between prices across different regions in a province.
- Prices published by Cement.com, a respected data source in the industry, show that WCC's market price is in fact a premium over its peers.
- WCC is able to command a price premium because (1) it is strategically located in Xi'an, and (2) it enjoys a monopoly in southern Shaanxi. While there are many other players in southern Shaanxi, the majority of them are subscale plants with high production costs and low energy efficiency. They also lack the ability to produce clinker, a material necessary for the production of cement, and typically purchase it from WCC.
- While its primary input costs are indeed in line with peers, WCC has initiated a number of cost-saving initiatives that lower cost of goods sold (COGS) and operating expenses.

Warning Signs

- WCC's selling prices were on average 3 percent lower than the average selling prices for cement in Shaanxi province from 2008 to 2011, while its costs were in line with the industry. It is highly unlikely for WCC to achieve margins that are significantly above peers.
- While WCC claims to have a market-leading position in Shaanxi, Glaucus's research showed that there are over 85 players in the region, many of which are located in the south and east, where WCC allegedly dominates. Hence, WCC is misrepresenting its market share.
- Shaanxi cement prices fell to new lows in the second half of 2011 and early 2012, while coal input costs were hitting new highs. Overcapacity led to a price war and heavy losses for Shaanxi's cement companies.
- WCC's competitors were acquiring other Shaanxi cement factories at RMB60 per ton. However, WCC paid an average of RMB349 per ton for its acquisitions, representing a 479 percent premium.
- The chairman of WCC's audit committee, Lee Kong Wai Conway, served on the audit committee of scandal-ridden Sino Vanadium.
- Ma Zhaoyang, an independent director of WCC, was the former chairman of Sino Vanadium.
- WCC's company secretary, Eric Sin Lik Man, was responsible for corporate governance at Norstar Founders Group Limited between 2007 and 2010. Trading of Norstar's stock has been halted for years after it lost nearly 80 percent of its value in 2008 under suspicion of fraud.

EBITDA Margins versus A-Share Comps

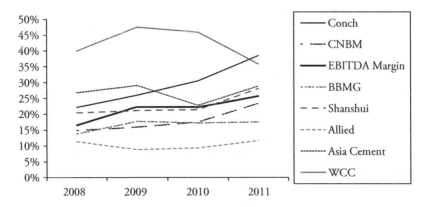

- WCC has had four different auditors in four years. In particular, PricewaterhouseCoopers (PwC) HK resigned after only four months, citing an inability to come to terms on the audit fee for FY2011.

Key Lessons

- When a company has poor corporate governance, additional scrutiny must be conducted when analyzing their financial data.
- Be wary of margins that are out of line with peer companies.

Case Study 4.3: China Biotics (CHBT US)

Background

- China Biotics is a Shanghai-based maker of food-supplement products. The company went public in the United States through a reverse merger in 2006 and was up-listed to Nasdaq in October 2008.
- The company engages in the research, development, production, marketing, and distribution of probiotics products. These products contain live bacteria, which act as dietary supplements and food additives to improve intestinal health and digestion.
- China Biotics' business consists of two segments: *retail probiotics products* and *bulk probiotics additives*.
- The retail business targeted the end consumers from large supermarkets and convenience stores, while the bulk business focused on institutional clients in the dairy and animal-feed industries.
- China Biotics products came in the form of an acidophilus pill. The industry is mature, with low but stable margins.
- China Biotics' stock price reached a high of about $19 in March 2010, with its highest market capitalization of approximately US$400 million. It has since plunged, closing at $3.46 before the Nasdaq halted trading in June 2011.
- At first glance, China Biotics' financials looked promising. In FY2010 (April 2009 to March 2010), total sales revenue reached US$81.4 million, up 50 percent year over year, while gross margin reached 70 percent.
- It seemed that China Biotics was cash rich, as the company stated cash of US$132 million (approximately $6/share in cash). This was more than 150 percent of Biotics' market value before it was halted on Nasdaq.
- The company attracted interest from major U.S. institutional money, including Wellington Management, which took an 8.2 percent stake in the company. Wellington no longer holds a stake at present.
- China Biotics' auditor was BDO Limited (Hong Kong–based affiliate of global accounting firm BDO International).

- Major shareholders of the company:
  - Song Jinan: 23 percent (ex-CFO and current CEO/chairman)
  - Azar Richard Essa: 18.1 percent
  - Kwok Leung Tai: 5.3 percent
  - Pope Investments: 3.4 percent
- The board of directors are:
  - Song Jinan (ex-CFO and current CEO/chairman)
  - Chin Ji Wei
  - Du Wen Min
  - Simon Yick
    Chin Ji Wei, Du Wen Min, and Simon Yick are independent directors.

What Happened

- In early 2009, short-sellers took note of China Biotics for two reasons: uncommonly wide profit margins (70 percent gross margins when it first came public) and large discrepancies between the company's financial reports filed with the SEC and SAIC.
- In 2010, private investigators hired by short-sellers allegedly discovered many of the stores China Biotics claimed to own in and around Shanghai did not exist.
- China Biotics responded that it had already closed down those stores after a strategic decision to shift to bulk wholesale probiotic sales. However, there still remained to be seen the true extent of the Biotics' manufacturing capabilities and the validity of its supply arrangements with certain customers.
- In March 2011, BDO Limited alleged that China Biotics had an elaborate scheme where it directed the auditors to a "suspected fake website" of China Biotics' bank (Bank of Communication) when BDO attempted to verify the firm's cash balance. BDO also noted irregularities involving interest income and the chops (used to verify document authenticity) that were included on a sales contract.
- BDO Limited had served as China Biotics' auditor for the last two audit cycles (FY2009 and 2010), though it refused to certify the FY2011 numbers. BDO's resignation was dated June 22, 2011.
- In June 2011, China Biotics' CFO, Travis Cai, resigned. A replacement was named: Marie Yang, the financial manager of one of China-Biotics' subsidiaries.
- On 15 June 2011, trading in China Biotics was halted on Nasdaq when the company failed to file its 10-K annual report with the SEC, due to missing the deadline for companies with fiscal years that end in March.
- China Biotics' stock had traded about $17 per share in January 2011, and dropped to $3.46 when the shares were delisted from Nasdaq in June. More

recently, the stock traded over the counter at $1.35, with market capitalization of about US$31 million.

Warning Signs

• *FY2010 annual report showed abnormally low inventory of only 12 days.* CHBT had inventory of 12 days in 2010 and only 9 days for 2008, which did not fit its manufacturing business model, with stated revenues of US$81 million in FY2010.

USD	2010.04-09	2010	2009	2008	2007	2006	2005
Operating Expense	16,119,083	24,070,203	16,197,267	12,310,092	8,910,633	6,445,148	4,419,649
Inventory	982,751	1,100,707	563,853	408,358	203,054	257,584	442,109
Inventory Turnover	15.47	28.92	33.32	40.27	38.69	18.42	19.99
Inventory Days	11.63	12.45	10.80	8.94	9.31	19.54	18.01

• *The company exaggerated the number of retail outlets.* China Biotics' FY2010 SEC Form 10-K stated it had 70 dedicated retail outlets in Shanghai, though investigative research on the ground found that only six outlets existed in Shanghai. Further, checks with selected supermarkets in Shanghai confirmed they had never carried "Double Gold probiotics," which was CHBT's main product.
• China Biotics' bulk additive business was grossly exaggerated. China Biotics stated FY2010 revenue of US$81 million, with 26.8 percent of revenue from bulk additives (approximately $21.7 million) and 73.2 percent from retail.

  However, checks with the Consulting Committee of China Healthcare Association revealed no large-scale probiotics domestic manufacturers, and the only known market leaders were Danisco (a Danish company recently acquired by DuPont) and Grape King (a Taiwanese company).

  China Biotics claimed it provided bulk additives to large dairy companies Yili, Mengniu, and Bright, though Yili denied using China Biotics as its supplier and Bright claimed it used its own probiotics.
• *The company's tax payable amount indicated exaggerated revenue and profit.* China Biotics accumulated approximately US$30.5 million in tax payable for FY2010, which was about 60 percent of all its tax to date.

USD	2010-04-09	2010	2009	2008	2007	2006	2005	Total
Revenue	48,524,366	81,363,973	54,197,082	42,321,111	30,609,941	21,862,385	14,421,772	109,215,209
Gross Profit	32,405,283	57,293,770	37,999,815	30,011,019	21,699,308	15,417,217	10,002,123	77,129,667
Net Profit	29,695,463	15,647,961	19,966,889	17,542,244	10,904,986	8,353,968	5,459,410	42,260,608
VAT	5,508,898	9,739,941	6,459,969	5,101,873	3,688,882	2,620,930	1,700,361	34,820,854
Income Tax	4,227,256	7,788,348	5,162,388	4,936,631	4,186,868	3,900,541	2,573,950	15,597,990
Total Tax	9,736,154	17,528,289	11,622,357	10,038,504	7,875,750	6,521,471	4,274,311	50,418,844
Tax Payable	30,572,679	28,989,337	25,528,447	22,317,982	18,009,721	15,316,318	11,132,621	N/A
Cash	158,843,559	155,579,371	70,824,041	64,310,448	26,992,025	19,840,812	10,271,503	N/A
Assets	253,798,072	232,934,682	120,804,347	93,791,526	44,579,844	33,426,988	21,245,378	N/A
Cash/Assets	62.59%	66.79%	58.63%	68.57%	60.55%	59.36%	48.35%	N/A

However, the company's claim of exemption of value-added tax was uncommon for health care product companies. It was unlikely for tax authorities to allow such a high amount on the books.

Biotics explained these were not real tax liabilities, but tax accrual in the event that the tax exemptions from five years ago were not approved.

A likely explanation could be that Biotics massively exaggerated its revenue and profit, therefore not paying the appropriate tax level for the exaggerated number.

Key Lessons

- The illusion of CHBT's large cash balance formed the core of investors' bullish hopes for dividends, and share buybacks. However, it was local sources in China that helped raise red flags on China Biotics.

  Allowing for further research into local Chinese websites, and finding news on the local papers would give added color on the business conduct of a company. This gives an added dimension on top of solely looking at the numbers.
- China Biotics had seen five CFOs in four years, with the first CFO, Song Jinan (major shareholder), in the post for only eight months (from March to November 2006). The fifth CFO, Travis Cai, served for a year and a half.

  Looking at the rate of change in a company's CFO lineup will post questions to an investor.

REFERENCES

China Biotics, Form 10-K for fiscal year ended March 31, 2011.
Eden, Scott. 2011. "Big Time Investors Lose Big on China." www.thestreet.com, June 23.
Glaucus Report on West China Cement.
Harbin Electric. Annual Reports for 2008 to 2010.
West China Cement. Annual Reports for 2009 to 2012.

CHAPTER 5

DETECTING
OVERSTATED
OPERATING
CASH FLOWS*

This chapter examines how companies may massage reported numbers to inflate some measure of cash flow such as operating cash flow. Often, but not always, this accompanies an overstatement of earnings as presented in earlier chapters. The chapter provides a checklist of analysis techniques and warnings signs to help you detect cash flow manipulation.

While accrual accounting and the income statement essentially reflect the economic activity and profitability of the period, a company cannot pay employees, creditors, and others with accrual-based net income; for this, an understanding of cash flows is necessary. Valuation models used in financial analysis are often based on projections of future cash flows as they depict the day-to-day operational financial viability of a business. Analysts would like to know the sources and uses of cash, particularly whether cash flow is derived from operating, investing, or financing activities. Some analysts use cash flow as a check on the quality of earnings. If a company is massaging its income statement to inflate income, this can be discovered by looking at the cash flow statement to see if it supports the strong income

---

*Portions of this chapter were adapted from Thomas R. Robinson, Paul Munter, and Julia Grant, *Financial Statement Analysis: A Global Approach* (Upper Saddle River, NJ: Prentice Hall, 2003), with permission.

or contradicts it. There have been many cases where a company reports strong and rising earnings coupled with negative cash flows, which have turned out to be accounting frauds.

Nevertheless, the cash flow statement is not infallible and can be manipulated. As with net income, management can have incentives to make cash flow look stronger than it really is. They may achieve this by engaging in real activities that accelerate cash flow into the current period such as by selling receivables to a third party. Another possibility is to slow down payments to suppliers. While neither of these practices is improper, the short-term boost to cash flow should be viewed skeptically since, effectively, the company is borrowing from its future.

However, the company may try to make cash flow look stronger than it really is by misclassifying cash flow. The cash flow statement is composed of three sections: operating, investing, and financing. Analysts would like to see the company generating positive operating cash flow and use this cash flow either to invest for the future (investing) or return this capital to investors or creditors (financing). A company can try to make itself look better by trying to classify cash receipts as operating activities (rather than, say, financing) or classifying cash payments as investing activities (rather than operating). For example, a company might borrow money from a creditor using accounts receivable as collateral and report this as a sale of the receivables (operating) rather than a borrowing transaction. The difference between an outright sale and a loan is real. In the case of a sale, the buyer should not have recourse against the seller if all of the receivables are not collected. However, in the borrowing transaction, the company is still obligated for any noncollectible accounts. Another method would be to classify a normal operating expenditure as a capital expenditure, as described in Chapter 2. In this manner, operating cash flow is overstated and investing cash flow is understated (larger cash outflows for capital expenditures).

UNDERSTANDING THE CASH FLOW STATEMENT

While the accrual accounting disclosures on the income statement provide rather accurate representations of a company's revenue and expense activities during the period, they do not necessarily provide a complete foundation for analysis and projections of cash flows. In fact, the income statement provides no indication of how a firm is managing cash. The cash flow statement provides the necessary additional information to supplement the information in the income statement. The cash flow statement for a hypothetical company is provided in Exhibit 5.1.

We have shown previously that the financial statements are all related. Both the income statement and the cash flow statement present flows of resources that occur between balance sheet dates, but the resources are measured differently in each statement. The income statement summarizes the changes in the retained earnings section of owners' equity, while the cash flow statement summarizes the changes in

EXHIBIT 5.1 Hypothetical Company Cash Flow Statement for the Month Ended 31 January 2013

Operating Activities	
Cash collected from customers	$ 20,000
Cash paid for rent	(2,000)
Cash paid to employees	(3,000)
Cash paid for utilities	(2,000)
Cash flow from operating activities	$ 13,000
Investing Activities	
Purchase of equipment	$ (60,000)
Purchase of securities	(3,000)
Sale of securities	3,500
Cash flow from investing activities	$ (59,500)
Financing Activities	
Issuance of stock	$200,000
Increase in notes payable	50,000
Repurchase of treasury stock	(100)
Cash flow from financing activities	$249,900
Total cash flow	$203,400
Beginning cash	0
Ending cash	$203,400

the cash accounts during the period. For the insightful analyst, the two statements, when used together, will provide valuable information. As such, an understanding of the relationships between the two statements is essential to the analyst.

Both the cash flow statement and the income statement are based on historical information, providing a means to directly evaluate management's past performance. Further, in combination with the balance sheet, these statements provide a means for estimating future cash flows (for example, collection of accounts receivable and payment of liabilities).

The cash flow statement required under U.S. generally accepted accounting principles (GAAP) or International Financial Reporting Standards (IFRS) presents a detailed display of what has caused the firm's cash and cash equivalents to change throughout a reporting period. Cash equivalents include investments that are readily convertible to a specified amount of cash. Under both standards, the net change in this class of assets over the reporting period is subdivided into three components: cash from operating activities, cash from investing activities, and cash from financing activities. These three components can be seen in the cash flow statement for a hypothetical company in Exhibit 5.1.

Each change in cash (or cash equivalents) is placed into one of the three areas under U.S. GAAP rules. IFRS offers some choices for specific items, which will be discussed later. Under either IFRS or U.S. GAAP, the full cash flow statement summarizes the change in cash and cash equivalents, reconciling the cash balance on the ending balance sheet with the beginning balance sheet. The net change is the sum of the effects of the three components—operating, investing, and financing.

Changes in cash occur as a result of either operating activities or financing and investing activities needed to maintain a firm's capital asset base. In a healthy, mature firm, operating activities should support themselves; that is, sales to customers should generate enough cash to pay for inventories sold to those customers and other operating expenses required to make those sales, such as wages. Investing activities, such as the acquisition and disposal of the long-term assets needed for operations, could be supported using excess cash from operations. Alternatively, the funds for these investments may be acquired by issuing debt or equity. These debt and equity transactions are the firm's financing activities.

In a new or rapidly growing firm, operating activities may not yet generate enough cash flow to support themselves without borrowing or issuing equity. However, a mature firm should not need to finance the current level of operations through debt or equity issuance. For a company to survive over the long run, its operations must be self-sustaining. Otherwise, the firm will ultimately have to take on excessive debt, eventually rendering it impossible for the company to issue further debt or equity. Should this persist, bankruptcy will occur. Consequently, it is important to have a clear picture of how the firm is managing its cash, in order to have an overall understanding of a company's financial position.

The cash flow statement begins with the operating activities section. Operating activities generally reflect cash generated and/or paid as a result of the firm's core business functions. This section of the cash flow statement is the cash counterpart to income from operations as reported on the income statement. As such, it provides a useful comparison and contrast to the accrual accounting measures on the income statement, potentially highlighting the effects of accrual accounting assumptions. Under U.S. GAAP, this category incorporates the cash received from customers, interest or dividends, and paid to suppliers, for operating costs, income taxes, and periodic interest costs.

While cash payments for interest are included in the operating activities section, under U.S. GAAP, dividends paid out to equity capital holders are reported in the financing section. Therefore, interest payments and dividend payments appear in different sections of the cash flow statement under U.S. GAAP. IFRS handles this issue differently, allowing the reporting company the option of including both interest and/or dividends in either operating or financing activities. Unlike the payment of interest expense, repayment of principal amounts to both debt and equity capital providers are treated as financing activities, which will be further discussed below.

The investing section of the cash flow statement presents cash transactions involving the typical noncurrent capital assets used in the firm's operations, such as property, plant, and equipment (PP&E) and intangible assets. The cash acquisitions of these assets result in cash outflows. Disposals of these types of assets for cash generate inflows. Note that the investing activities section does not necessarily provide a complete listing of all capital asset activity because only acquisitions or disposals involving cash appear here. Noncash acquisitions, such as acquisition of a building using a mortgage, are disclosed in supplemental information to the cash flow statement.

The financing section of the cash flow statement shows the long-term inflow and outflow of capital to the firm in the form of cash from investors. These include both equity investments of stockholders (owners) and loans from bondholders and other creditors, detailing both the increases in cash resulting from the initial investments made by these parties and decreases in cash resulting from any money paid to stockholders in the form of dividends (in U.S. GAAP), outflows for repurchase of stock (treasury stock), and principal payments to bondholders and other creditors. This section of the cash flow statement is typically related to activities in the noncurrent liabilities and owners' equity section of the balance sheet. Remember that under IFRS, cash interest payments may also be included here.

The cash flow statement summarizes all cash account activities of the corporation, essentially depicting the firm's bank statements for the year, sorting all transactions and summarizing them into categories. The checks would be sorted by what type of bill was being paid, the deposits would be sorted by the source of the inflow, and the resulting statement would create a cash flow statement in what is called the *direct method format*. This is the format presented earlier for our hypothetical company.

In the direct method format (as shown in Exhibit 5.1), each line of the operating activities section represents a sum of all checks or deposits in a particular category. For example, the operating activities section would include such items as cash received from customers; cash paid to suppliers; cash paid for interest; cash paid for wages; cash paid for research and development; cash paid for selling, general and administrative costs; and any other relevant summary lines.

The investing activities section would include such items as cash paid for acquiring capital assets and cash received from disposal of the same classes of assets. Also included in this section would be the cash paid to invest in the stock of another firm, as well as the proceeds from the subsequent sale of the stock.

The financing activities section would include cash received from stockholders' investments in the firm and any cash returned to stockholders, whether in the form of stock repurchases or dividends paid. The liability component of financing activities would include cash received from debtholders who have loaned money to the firm during the period less any principal payments made by the firm back to those debtholders.

Both U.S. GAAP and IFRS encourage companies to present operating cash flows using the direct method format, but another method, the indirect method, is also available. The direct method would provide the summarized details from the cash account, as described earlier, corresponding to deposits made and checks written. The items in this intuitive format are straightforward and easy for the analyst to understand. In fact, under both IFRS and U.S. GAAP, the financing and investing activities sections are presented in just this manner.

While expressing the preference for the direct method, U.S. GAAP and IFRS also include the requirement that when the direct method is presented for the cash flow statement, the notes to the statement must include a reconciliation of accrual accounting net income to cash from operating activities. This reconciliation constitutes the indirect method format. Our hypothetical company's cash flow statement, using the indirect method, is presented in Exhibit 5.2.

Companies may choose to do one of the following:

- Report the cash flow statement under the direct method, with an indirect reconciliation provided as supplementary information.
- Report the cash flow statement under the indirect method.

Understandably, most firms opt to create only one format, the indirect method, and present it on the face of the cash flow statement. Only rarely does a firm provide the direct method format.

This indirect format links the cash from operating activities to the accrual accounting income statement results, clarifying the distinction between the two. The income statement reflects the operations of the firm, measured on the accrual basis, rather than on a cash basis. Most of the items in an income statement are related to operating activities as defined by the cash flow statement rules. Therefore, it is possible to reconcile the net income from the income statement to the cash from operating activities. This is accomplished by removing the effects of items that appear on the income statement but do not affect cash such as depreciation and amortization expense, items where the timing between accrual and cash is different (e.g., changes in accounts receivable, accounts payable, prepaids) as well as a few items that appear on the income statement but are not categorized as operating activities for cash flow purposes (e.g., gains or losses from sale of PP&E—remember, cash flows from sale of PP&E are included in the investing activities section). This format can actually help the analysts identify areas where net income has increased artificially, as it will appear as a reduction to net income in arriving at operating cash flow.

EXHIBIT 5.2   Hypothetical Company Cash Flow Statement for the Month Ended 31 January 2013

Operating Activities	
Net income	$7,000
Plus depreciation expense	1,000
Less gain on sale of stock	(500)
Less increase in accounts receivable	(10,000)
Less increase in inventory	(5,000)
Plus increase in accounts payable	20,000
Plus increase in interest payable	500
Cash flow from operating activities	$ 13,000
Investing Activities	
Purchase of equipment	$(60,000)
Purchase of securities	(3,000)
Sale of securities	3,500
Cash flow from investing activities	$ (59,500)
Financing Activities	
Issuance of stock	$200,000
Increase in notes payable	50,000
Repurchase of treasury stock	(100)
Cash flow from financing activities	$ 249,900
Total cash flow	$ 203,400
Beginning cash	0
Ending cash	$ 203,400

USING CASH FLOW TO ASSESS THE QUALITY OF EARNINGS

Cash flow–based ratios have become increasingly popular in recent years. As noted earlier, while accounting profits are nice, employees, creditors, and investors prefer to get paid in cash. Additionally, some firms have been aggressive in reporting earnings, and an examination of cash flow ratios can provide insight on the quality of a firm's earnings. You can replace earnings in virtually any ratio with some measure of cash flow. In this section, we highlight some useful cash flow–based ratios.

A firm's profitability on a cash flow basis relative to sales can be computed as an operating cash margin:

Cash Flow from Operating Activities/Sales Revenue

- The ratio presents the percentage of revenue reflected in operating cash flow. A ratio of 5 percent indicates that the firm is generating $5 of cash flow from operating activities for every $100 of sales.
- Similarly, we can compute a cash return on assets as:

Cash Flow from Operating Activities/Average Total Assets

- A result of 10 percent would indicate that the firm is generating $10 of operating cash flow for every $100 of total assets.

Taken together, the preceding ratios assess the company's ability to generate cash flow. Comparing these ratios to their earnings-based equivalents also provides insight into the quality of the company's earnings. For example, if the earnings-based ratios show strong profitability but the cash flow–based ratios show an inability to generate cash flow, this could indicate poor earnings quality. However, it can also be indicative of a rapidly growing firm, so this analysis should serve only as a starting point. If earnings and cash-based ratios are out of sync, you should take a closer look at accounting methods and estimates used by the firm.

Another way to examine earnings quality using cash flow is to compare cash flow from operating activities to net income. This can be done in currency or by creating a cash flow–earnings index:

Cash Flow from Operating Activities/Net Income

In any one year, this ratio can be higher or lower than 1. Over the long term, however, the ratio should exceed 1. This is due to the fact that noncash charges (primarily depreciation) are deducted from net income but do not represent an operating cash outflow. In fact, the cash flow related to depreciable assets occurs when the asset is acquired and is classified as an investing cash outflow. As with the preceding discussion, if this ratio is consistently below 1 or declining, it is indicative of a potential problem with earnings quality. Should this occur, special attention must be paid to accounting issues.

Ideally, a firm's operating cash flow should be sufficient to pay for capital expenditures. A firm's free cash flow can be computed as:

Cash Flow from Operating Activities − Capital Expenditures

A positive value indicates the existence of free cash flow, operating cash flows in excess of those needed.

Application: Renhe Commercial Holdings

Renhe Commercial Holdings is a developer of underground shopping centers in China. The company installs furniture, fixtures, and equipment (FF&E) in government-owned underground bomb shelters in densely populated areas. Renhe retains the right to use the property for commercial purposes, though it does not own the real estate due to legal issues (as it is for civil defense use). In 2010 and 2011, it reported large and increasing net profits. Following is the operating section of Renhe's cash flow statement from the 2011 annual report.

	2011	2010
	RMB (thousands)	RMB (thousands)
Operating activities		
Profit for the year	5,439,287	3,654,412
Adjustments for:		
Depreciation	29,913	22,692
Net finance expenses	457,240	291,866
Loss on disposal of property and equipment	47	102
Gain on disposal of investment properties	(6,512)	—
Net gain on disposal of subsidiaries	(8,762)	(3,431,389)
Change in fair value of investment properties	(6,867,322)	(1,333,182)
Income tax	1,987,110	248,052
Operating profit before changes in working capital	1,031,001	(547,447)
(Increase)/decrease in bank deposits	(184,083)	306,562
Increase in trade and other receivables	(638,605)	(1,063,576)
Increase in trade and other payables	189,448	3,115,135
Decrease in inventories	824,757	153,485
Income tax paid	(203,267)	(474,855)
Net cash generated from operating activities	1,019,251	1,489,304

Note that while profits are large and increasing, operating cash flow is small and decreasing. This disconnect indicates a potential problem. Note the negative

(Continued)

(*Continued*)

adjustments for receivables and change in fair value of investment properties. These two items explain a large portion of the difference between profit and cash flows and are worrisome. They show that all profits in reality came from an alleged increase in value of investment properties, and the increase in receivables indicates a potential problem with collection of receivables.

CASH FLOW GAMES

Typical cash flow games are aimed at increasing either total cash flow or the subtotal for operating cash flow since that is a key indicator of value for a company. As noted earlier, companies can do this by either engaging in real activities that temporarily boost current cash flow but reverse in the future or misclassifying activities such that cash flow is overstated.

Engaging in real activities to boost current cash flow can be done by accelerating cash receipts into the current year or delaying cash payments to later years. Typical activities include:

- Aggressive encouragement of customers to pay their balances sooner than required.
- Sale of accounts receivable in a factoring arrangement (outright sale where receivables are sold at a discount and without recourse).
- Delaying payments to suppliers, employees, and others.

These types of activities can be found by looking at the reconciliation items between net income and the cash flow statement for items that increase cash flow more than in normal periods. You should consider the impact of these activities when estimating long-term expected cash flow even though they are not improper.

Another real activity that companies engage in related to cash flow is not a cash flow at all but can impact valuation measures such as free cash flow. This activity is the purchase of PP&E on credit. Effectively, the company is borrowing cash (a financing cash inflow) and purchasing equipment (an investing cash outflow), but if the transaction is structured as a direct borrowing transaction, it will bypass the cash flow statement. These transactions must be disclosed in the footnotes, so a review of the footnotes is essential to detect them and properly estimate measures like free cash flow.

Artificial means of inflating operating cash flow include a variety of activities. One simple example relates to the sale of receivables activity mentioned above. If the company transfers accounts receivables to another company, which becomes liable for any collection problems (known as a transfer with recourse), then it is not really a sale. Instead, it is a borrowing transaction, and the cash inflow should appear in the financing section rather than the operating section. The accounts receivable quantum remains on the balance sheet in this case. Companies may try to disguise these transactions as a sale without recourse and improperly classify the cash inflow as an operating activity rather than a financing activity.

Companies can take this type of scenario one step further by engaging in activities that convert (improperly) any borrowing from a financing cash flow into an operating cash flow. The American company Enron did this by using financial firms to create a series of special-purpose entities that were effectively borrowing funds and "laundering" them through these other entities and recording as both operating income and operating cash flow. You should examine footnote disclosures and uses of special-purpose entities to explore any unusual financing-type activities.

A common method to boost operating cash flow used by companies, such as WorldCom, is to misclassify normal operating expenses as capital expenditures. This simultaneously boosts operating income and operating cash flow.

Application: Sino-Forest

Recall the Sino-Forest discussion in previous chapters. In addition to revenue manipulation, Sino-Forest reported purchases of trees as capital expenditures rather than inventory. They therefore appeared as an investing cash outflow rather than an operating cash outflow.

US$ m	2010	2009	2008	2007
Revenues	1,924	1,238	901	714
Net Income	395	286	229	152
Cash Flow from Operations before Δ in Working Capital	1,174	826	542	456
Δ in Accounts Receivable	(346)	(59)	(111)	24
Δ in Other Working Capital	12	17	53	7
Net Cash Flow from Operations	840	784	483	486
Additions to Timber Holdings	(1,359)	(1,032)	(657)	(640)
Other Investing Expenditure	(43)	(36)	(47)	(52)
Cash Flow before Financing	(562)	(285)	(221)	(206)

Note that while operating cash flow was overstated by this activity, free cash flow was not. Since free cash flow is operating cash flow less capital expenditures, it is a very useful check on this type of activity.

EXHIBIT 5.3   Cash Flow Warning Signs

Acceleration of Cash Received for Revenues or Deferral of Cash Paid for Expenses	• Look for factoring, sales of receivables, or other transactions to bring cash flow in early. • See if the company is delaying payments to suppliers and others, such as an increase in accounts payable.
Borrowing Transactions Treated as Operating Cash Inflow	• Are there contingent or other off-balance-sheet liabilities disclosed (or not disclosed)? • Look for reciprocal or repurchase agreements/insurance-type contracts. • Is there any revenue from an unusual type of customer (financial services firm)?
Expenditures Improperly Classified as Capital Expenditures	• Are there abnormal increases in long-term assets? • Are there unusual assets? • Any abnormal changes in capital expenditures?

PARTING COMMENTS

The cash flow statement is as important, if not more important, to the analyst than the income statement. Cash flow is essential to the operation and valuation of the business. The cash flow statement also provides a very good check against the quality of reported income. Management can, however, manipulate reported cash flow. A checklist of warning signs is provided in Exhibit 5.3.

CASE STUDIES

The following cases examine companies that may have been accused—but not necessarily ascertained guilty—of manipulating their reported results. These cases demonstrate many of the concepts presented in this chapter. Note that some concepts in these cases may be related to concepts covered in other chapters; however the full case is included for completeness and to demonstrate that there is often a plural nature of accounting manipulation.

Case Study 5.1: Renhe Commercial Holdings

Background

• Renhe Commercial Holdings is a developer of underground shopping centres in China. The company installs FF&E in government-owned underground bomb shelters in densely populated areas. Renhe retains the right to use the property for commercial purposes, though it does not own the real estate due to legal issues (as it is for civil defense use).

- An initial public offering (IPO) was held in October 2008 by UBS, HSBC, MS, and BOCI for 3 billion shares at HKD 1.13, with current market capitalization of approximately HKD 7.61 billion. The stock price hit a high of HKD 2.25 in February 2009 and a low of HKD 0.33 in May 2012. The stock was currently trading at HKD 0.38 as of June 2012.

- In FY2011, Renhe saw revenue growth of +96 percent, at RMB2.24 billion, and its profit before-tax was a healthy RMB7.43 billion, an increase of 90.3 percent from fiscal year 2010.

- Operating cash flows were a positive RMB1.02 billion from operating activities, with net cash and cash equivalents at RMB1.88 billion.

- Renhe issued two bonds with a total face value of US$900 million, with the first due May 2015 (US$300 million with a 11.75 percent coupon), and the second due March 2016 (US$600 million with a 13 percent coupon).

- Renhe's auditor was KPMG.

- Major shareholders of the company:
  - Super Brilliant Investment: 48.5 percent
  - Atlantis Investment: 6 percent
  - Capital International: 5.1 percent
  - JPMorgan Chase: 4.97 percent
  - Norges Bank: 4.92 percent

- Mrs. Hawken Xiu Li (one of the non-executive directors, and sister of Chairman Dai Yongge) owns Shining Hill, which in turn owns Super Brilliant, which holds the 48.5 percent stake in Renhe.

- The board of directors involved:
  - Dai Yongge (chairman)
  - Hawken Xiu Li (non-executive director/chairman's sister)
  - Executive directors:
    Zhang Dabin (wholly owns United Magic Ltd.)
    Wang Hongfang (wholly owns Swift Fast Ltd.)
    Wang Chunrong (wholly owns Wonder Future Ltd.)
    Wang Luding (wholly owns Wisdom High Ltd.)
  - Renhe granted 80,000,000 share options at exercise price HKD 1.69 on 8 February 2010, to each of the four companies that the four executive directors wholly own.

- In March 2009, secondary placements of 450 million shares at HKD 1.68 were placed out by BOCI and UBS, followed by 400 million shares at HKD 1.70 by Morgan Stanley in April 2009.

- In July 2009, Renhe and controlling shareholder Super Brilliant raised HKD 5.58 billion in a private share sale.

Both entered into a placing agreement with UBS to procure purchasers for 3 billion shares at HKD 1.86 to six independent investors. At that time, the 3 billion placing shares represented approximately 15 percent of the issued share capital of Renhe.

Out of the 3 billion shares, proceeds from 1 billion shares owned by controlling shareholder Hawken Li was used to invest in her family's agricultural wholesale business (not part of the listed company), China Shouguang Agricultural.

Pursuant to the placing asgreement, Super Brilliant conditionally agreed to subscribe for 2 billion new shares at the placing price of HKD 1.86. The proceeds from the subscription amount, approximately HKD 3.58 billion, was used for the acquisition of operation rights for five projects in Weifang, Chengdu, Dalian, Anshan Phase, and Daqing.

Warning Signs

- In FY2010 and 2011, Renhe announced lackluster sales for the first nine months of the year before later announcing that sales targets were met in the fourth quarter, with huge accounts receivables. This happened for both consecutive years.

  In addition, the high gross profit margins of approximately 70 percent were seen to be unsustainable in the face of growing competition (despite Renhe's stating average construction costs of RMB8,400 per square meter).

  Renhe did not disclose the purchasers' identities, which is unusual, especially when the amount owed to Renhe is HKD 4.6 billion. On the buyer's side, CC Land did not show either purchase or payable on its 2010 financials.
- The people in charge of the Weifang project (Weifang Renhe New World Public Facilities Co. Ltd:
  - How Mun Lam (Peter) is chairman and GM of New World, and is also deputy chairman and MD of CC Land.
  - Kwok Keung Kwong is a director of New World, and is also director of Nice Angel Ltd. It happens that Nice Angel shares the same office space with Yugang, CC Land's largest shareholder. Yugang and Nice Angel's office is next door to CC Land's office in the China Resources Building in Hong Kong.
  - Kwok and Peter How are also the secretary and director of a Hong Kong company (Fame Vantage) that owns New World.
  - CC Land Chairman Cheung is in turn Yugang's largest shareholder.
- Individual buying power lacked financial muscle to pay HKD 1.09 billion for Weifang.

  It is improbable that Peter How could have bought the Weifang project despite being well paid by CC Land (HKD 10 million annual salary). In addition, CC Land's Chairman Cheung, who denied personal involvement in the purchase, would have to liquidate his entire stake in CC in order to fund the Weifang purchase. He has not filed disclosure along those lines.

Based on the preceding, CC Land is the only probable buyer of Weifang at this point.

- Opacity in CC Land's payables and Renhe's accounts receivable:

  CC Land showed neither purchases nor payables in its 2010 financials and did not mention the Weifang underground mall in its property detail. Payables explanation in its accounts receivable did not mention the purchase or any balance large enough to compensate for the HKD 1.09 billion selling price Renhe reported.

  However, Renhe claims it had received payments against the disposals, without naming the amounts due on each individual project's disposal.

- The Weifang receivable is likely to be in default, as the supposed debtor—CC Land Holdings—did not disclose owing any amount or having made any payments on the project.

  If that happens, the Weifang receivable would be stated in Renhe's future accounts receivable as a bad receivable, which currently is approximately 14 percent of its outstanding offshore debt.

What Happened

- In March 2011, Renhe announced in its annual report that it had sold five projects in a series of offshore transactions, for total proceeds of HKD 4.6 billion. The five projects were Weifang, Chengdu, Dalian, Anshan Phase, and Daqing.

- Stock and bond investors viewed the announcement as a significant positive because it showed that Renhe could generate significant cash offshore to meet dividend and bond payments, despite having an unusual property-light real estate development model.

- The sales were largely made through seller financing, with Renhe recording significant receivables. The company claimed it received 30 percent up front (approximately HKD 1.4 billion for all five sales) and sold the projects by selling various British Virgin Islands (BVI) holding companies to the buyers' BVI holding companies.

- Renhe never disclosed the beneficial purchasers of the five projects.

- Of the five projects announced, Renhe stated the sale of its Weifang project would net HKD 1.09 billion, for which Renhe would receive 30 percent in accounts receivable (HKD 300 million).

- On 9 December 2011, the *Hong Kong Economic Journal* (HKEJ) reported that Mr. Cheung Chung Kiu (CC Land Holding's chairman) was the purchaser of a Renhe project in Chengdu and was in default of the purchase.

- The HKEJ report caused Renhe's share price to decline by 17 percent. Renhe filed a clarification announcement denying that either Mr. Cheung or CC Land had ever purchased any properties from Renhe.

- CC Land also responded, though with a significant difference. CC Land stated that neither CC Land nor Chairman Cheung was involved in the "project transaction" (i.e., Chengdu), and that Chairman Cheung did not acquire any related projects or any other Renhe Commercial project.

The difference: While Renhe maintained that CC Land and its chairman never bought any Renhe properties, CC Land stated only that it was not involved in the Chengdu project and that its chairman never bought any Renhe properties.

- In its annual report for FY2011, CC Land did not disclose owing any amount or having made any payments on the Weifang project.
- For FY2011, Renhe's sales of RMB2.2 billion were below Moody's expectation, with accounts receivables remaining high, at RMB4.8 billion, despite collection of sales proceeds from its disposal of BVI subsidiaries holding its projects.
- Rapid consumption of cash was also a concern, with cash balance dropping to RMB2.2 billion in December 2011 from RMB8.8 billion in 2010. This was due to the repurchase of shares totaling RMB1 billion, acquisition of the Wuxi project for RMB2.6 billion, construction costs of RMB4.6 billion, and dividend payments of RMB1.5 billion.
- Before the announcement of FY2011 results, Standard & Poor's downgraded Renhe to B+ from BB–, followed by Moody's downgrade to B3 from B1.
- In February 2012, Ripley Capital (a research house) put out a report stating that the Weifang project's site acquisitions were misrepresented by Renhe.

They charged that Renhe misled investors by telling them the site, split into three adjoining areas, could be combined into one large single block, which allowed for development in three phases. However, the three sites were actually more than 1.3 km apart from each other.

Further investigation found that leasing and retail business at the Weifang project was poor, with large spaces deserted. Merchants at the site mentioned poor foot traffic.

- At present, no official announcement has been made by the Hong Kong Exchange to show that Renhe misrepresented its accounts receivable in any of the five projects. However, in April 2013, Standard & Poor's lowered its credit rating on Renhe to CCC, citing that cash collections would not likely be sufficient to cover interest payments in the next 12 months.

Key Lessons

- It is important to know who the buyers of a company's products are, especially in the area of accounts receivables—even more so when the amounts are huge (HKD 4.6 billion)

The footnotes of Renhe's annual report for 2011 did not state any names of buyers. Research outside of the annual report (e.g., through existing customers) might provide clues to the potential buyers.
- Scrutiny of corporate governance:

The people in charge of Weifang Renhe New World Public Facilities (Peter How and Kwok) were intricately linked to CC Land, through Nice Angel, Yugang, and Fame Vantage.

Questions arose not only about how Peter How is chairman of New World and an MD of CC Land, but also about the issue of physical proximity between New World's office and CC Land.

It remains to be seen how Renhe would disentangle its accounts receivable from its alleged purchasers.

Case Study 5.2: Duoyuan Global Water (NYSE: DGW)

Background

- DGW is a New York Stock Exchange (NYSE)–listed company based in China with a market cap of US$135.11 million on 4 April 2011.
- It is a domestic water treatment equipment supplier whose products include circulating water treatment equipment, water purification equipment, and wastewater treatment equipment.
- The company is involved in the water treatment process, such as filtration, water softening, water sediment separation, aeration, disinfection, and reverse osmosis.
- 4 April 2011: Muddy Waters released a research report on DGW, alleging that the company was a fraud.
- Major shareholders as of 31 May 2010:
  Wenhua Guo (director, chairman, and CEO): 48.6 percent
  GEEMF III Holdings MU: 9.0 percent
- Auditor: Grant Thornton Hong Kong → BDO Hong Kong.
  - In November 2010, Grant Thornton International separated from its Hong Kong member firm, and over 600 partners and professionals from Grant Thornton Hong Kong moved to BDO
  - This follows the disappearance of Grant Thornton Hong Kong's managing partner Gabriel Azedo amid allegations that he stole over US$12.1 million from friends and clients. These events raised serious questions about the culture of Grant Thornton Hong Kong's office, and may partly explain the deficiencies in DGW's audits.
  - Following the merger between BDO and Grant Thornton Hong Kong, DGW has engaged BDO's Hong Kong office as its auditor.

What Happened

4 April 2011

- Muddy Waters LLC recommends a strong sell on DGW and estimates the company's value at less than US$1.00 per share. At that point in time, DGW was trading at US$5.49 per share. The following allegations were made:
  1. DGW's reported revenue of US$154.4 million is overstated by over 100 times. The company's actual revenue is estimated to be less than US$800,000 annually.
     - DGW's factory in Langfang, Hebei, was less a factory and more an adult day-care center. There were few signs of human activity, and Muddy Waters

counted only approximately 240 employees during its surveillance when DGW's F-1 stated that the company had 813 workers, with the chairman later revising that figure to 580.

- DGW's Beijing headquarters had only four employees (and many empty desks) when Muddy Waters visited their office. Contrary to disclosures in DGW's Securities and Exchange Commission (SEC) filings, companies with no affiliation to the Duoyuan Group rent the majority of the space in the building.

2. After Muddy Waters viewed DGW's People's Republic of China (PRC) audit report by Langfang Zhongtianjian, which substantiated their thesis, DGW apparently replaced its audit report with a forged one that was less incriminating.

3. Four errors were identified in DGW's U.S. audit, indicating that DGW's auditor, Grant Thornton Hong Kong, was sloppy and unreliable.

   a. Auditor sloppiness regarding DGW's purported rent payments to an entity that had already been merged into one of DGW's subsidiaries prior to the company's 2009 IPO.

   b. Auditor's failure to detect incorrect classification of purported property transfer on the cash flow statement, which was reported under operating cash flow instead of cash flow from investing. This boosted operating cash flow by RMB44.5 million in 2008, the year prior to DGW's IPO.

   c. Auditor's failure to detect incorrect classification on the cash flow statement of the loan Chairman Guo repaid in 2008, which was classified under operating cash flow instead of cash flow from financing activities. This boosted operating cash flow by RMB43.8 million in 2008, the year prior to DGW's IPO.

   d. Auditor's credulity about no work-in-process at year-end—Muddy Waters' manufacturing experts believe that this would be impossible if DGW were generating anywhere close to the level of revenue and year-on-year growth it claims.

4. DGW's distribution network of 80 distributors in 28 provinces is a sham.

5. DGW engages in improper undisclosed related-party transactions that transfer money to its chairman and CEO, Wenhua Guo.

   - DGW Langfang's 2009 audit report shows that it transferred money in undisclosed transactions to a company owned by Chairman Guo, Beijing Huiyuan Duoyuan Digital Printing Technology Institute (Huiyuan).

   - Huiyuan, a sole proprietorship, is a special type of legal entity that is particularly opaque, and hence well-suited for draining money from DGW.

- Chairman Guo attempted to obscure DGW Langfang's improper payables to Huiyuan by listing two different payables to Huiyuan using different Chinese characters (but having the same pronunciation) for Huiyuan's name. Huiyuan was alternately written in the 2009 audit report as 慧元研究所 and 惠元研究所. Muddy Waters has searched for the alternate entity, but there is none. Both names refer to the same entity, which Chairman Guo owns.
- DGW Langfang's 2009 audit report showed an accounts payable balance of RMB26.2 million at year-end, which was a growth of 434 percent from the previous year. This payable is far more than the revenue DGW Langfang generates, without a plausible reason for DGW to be doing business with Huiyuan, which claims to be in the printing business.
- Most important, DGW does not disclose these related-party transactions in its SEC filings.
- Despite Huiyuan's equity capital being de minimis, and recording no revenue in 2009 according to its State Administration of Industry & Commerce (SAIC) file, it has managed to make investments totaling at least RMB30.5 million in other entities over the years.
- Sister company Duoyuan Printing (DYP) has had numerous problems, including the dismissal of its auditor, Deloitte. The chairman of DYP, Wenhua Guo, is also DGW's chairman and CEO

May 2011

- Four of six independent directors resigned, citing management's refusal to provide information. A special investigative committee has been formed, which has engaged Baker & McKenzie and PricewaterhouseCoopers.

Warning Signs

- Look out for incorrect classifications in the cash flow statement.
- It is highly unlikely that a company with DGW's revenue stream and year-on-year growth would have no work-in-process at year-end.

Key Lessons

- Be wary of auditors with past records of fraud.
- Look for alternative objective evidence to support reported revenues through company visits or review of other regulatory filings.

Appendix

DUOYUAN GLOBAL WATER INC. AND SUBSIDIARIES
CONSOLIDATED BALANCE SHEETS

	31 December 2008	31 December 2009	31 December 2009
	RMB	RMB	US$
	ASSETS		
CURRENT ASSETS:			
Cash	198,518,061	918,667,261	$134,585,514
Accounts receivable	137,549,786	197,087,701	28,873,511
Inventories, net of reserve for obsolescence	46,726,339	33,419,900	4,896,043
Other receivables	46,500	676,376	99,089
Other current assets	645,376	1,344,702	197,000
Deposits	9,990,000	5,605,530	821,215
Total current assets	393,476,062	1,156,801,470	169,472,372
PLANT AND EQUIPMENT, net	117,681,359	144,755,275	21,206,768
OTHER ASSETS:			
Prepaid leases	22,481,491	21,957,806	3,216,837
Deposits — long term	—	44,378,173	6,501,439
Deferred tax assets	4,446,899	4,694,347	687,726
Total other assets	26,928,390	71,030,326	10,406,002
Total assets	538,085,811	1,372,587,071	$201,085,142
LIABILITIES AND SHAREHOLDERS' EQUITY			
CURRENT LIABILITIES:			
Notes payable	20,000,000	20,000,000	$2,930,017
Accounts payable	38,696,788	27,913,596	4,089,365
Other payables	24,927,232	19,722,465	2,889,357
Income taxes payable	10,768,521	15,423,292	2,259,525
Total current liabilities	94,392,541	83,059,353	12,168,264

	31 December 2008	31 December 2009	31 December 2009
	RMB	RMB	US$
SHAREHOLDERS' EQUITY:			
Ordinary shares, US$0.000033 par value: Authorized shares—1,500,000,000; Issued and outstanding—30,000,000 shares at 31 December 2008 and 43,702,631 shares at 31 December 2009	7,295	10,384	1,521
Additional paid-in capital	132,455,705	861,292,062	126,180,000
Statutory reserves	36,413,141	57,319,979	8,397,424
Retained earnings	274,817,129	370,905,293	54,337,933
Total shareholders' equity	443,693,270	1,289,527,718	188,916,878
Total liabilities and shareholders' equity	538,085,811	1,372,587,071	$201,085,142

DUOYUAN GLOBAL WATER INC. AND SUBSIDIARIES
CONSOLIDATED STATEMENTS OF CASH FLOWS

	YEAR ENDED 31 DECEMBER			
	2007	2008	2009	2009
	RMB	RMB	RMB	US$
CASH FLOWS FROM OPERATING ACTIVITIES:				
Net income	82,208,345	133,766,862	116,995,002	$17,139,865
Less: Net loss from discontinued operations	(179,767)	—	—	—
Net income from continuing operations	82,388,112	133,766,862	116,995,002	17,139,865
Adjustments to reconcile net income to cash provided by operating activities:				
Depreciation	8,254,977	8,711,905	10,664,776	1,562,399

(Continued)

DUOYUAN GLOBAL WATER INC. AND SUBSIDIARIES
CONSOLIDATED STATEMENTS OF CASH FLOWS (Continued)

	YEAR ENDED 31 DECEMBER			
	2007	2008	2009	2009
	RMB	RMB	RMB	US$
Amortization	245,833	384,756	523,685	76,720
Share-based compensation expense	—	—	91,256,413	13,369,140
Loss from sale of property	—	3,215,744	4,693	688
(Increase) decrease in assets:			Artificially boosted by 3b and c	
Accounts receivable	(41,102,815)	(5,141,423)	(59,537,915)	(8,722,354)
Inventories	40,123,010	(24,194,045)	13,306,439	1,949,404
Other receivables	2,206,304	178,028	(629,876)	(92,277)
Related party receivables	(58,539,020)	102,010,133	—	—
Deposits	1,143,085	(9,990,000)	(5,605,530)	(821,215)
Other current assets	—	(645,376)	(699,326)	(102,452)
Deferred tax assets	(101,974)	312,863	(247,448)	(36,251)
Other non-current assets	3,500,000	—	—	—
Increase (decrease) in liabilities:				
Accounts payable	11,528,690	19,055,433	(10,783,192)	(1,579,747)
Advances from customers	(3,893,249)	—	—	—
Deferred tax liabilities	(742,415)	—	—	—
Other payables	(2,069,639)	17,575,474	(5,204,767)	(762,503)
Related party payables	622,368	(622,368)	—	—
Taxes payable	3,088,475	(2,932,116)	4,654,771	681,928
Total operating cash flows provided by continuing operations	46,651,742	241,685,870	154,697,725	22,663,345
Discontinued operations	25,417,970	—	—	—
Total cash flows provided by operating activities	72,069,712	241,685,870	154,697,725	22,663,345

	YEAR ENDED 31 DECEMBER			
	2007	2008	2009	2009
	RMB	RMB	RMB	US$
CASH FLOWS FROM INVESTING ACTIVITIES:				
Deposits for purchase of land use rights	—	—	(5,320,000)	(779,384)
Deposits for purchase of equipment	—	—	(33,823,830)	(4,955,219)
Deposits for leasehold improvements	—	—	(5,234,343)	(766,836)
Purchase of building	(38,941,600)	(6,020,634)	—	—
Purchase of equipment and furniture	—	(16,200,000)	(27,753,385)	(4,065,894)
Total investing cash flows used in continuing operations	(38,941,600)	(22,220,634)	(72,131,558)	(10,567,333)
Discontinued operations	1,911,057	—	—	—
Total cash flows used in investing activities	(37,030,543)	(22,220,634)	(72,131,558)	(10,567,333)
CASH FLOWS FROM FINANCING ACTIVITIES:				
Payment of short-term notes, net	(15,000,000)	(49,000,000)	—	—
Proceeds from Initial Public Offering, net of offering costs	—	—	637,583,033	93,406,442
Total cash flows (used in) provided by financing activities	(15,000,000)	(49,000,000)	637,583,033	93,406,442
NET INCREASE IN CASH OF DISCONTINUED OPERATIONS	583,524	—	—	—

(Continued)

DUOYUAN GLOBAL WATER INC. AND SUBSIDIARIES
CONSOLIDATED STATEMENTS OF CASH FLOWS (Continued)

	YEAR ENDED 31 DECEMBER			
	2007	2008	2009	2009
	RMB	RMB	RMB	US$
INCREASE IN CASH	20,622,693	170,465,236	720,149,200	105,502,454
CASH, beginning of period	7,430,132	28,052,825	198,518,061	29,083,060
CASH, end of period	28,052,825	198,518,061	918,667,261	$134,585,514
SUPPLEMENTARY DISCLOSURE OF CASH FLOW INFORMATION:				
Cash paid during the period for:				
Income taxes	10,612,162	40,449,769	66,863,315	$9,795,531
Interest	5,759,416	3,117,818	1,218,745	$178,547

Corporate Structure of DGW

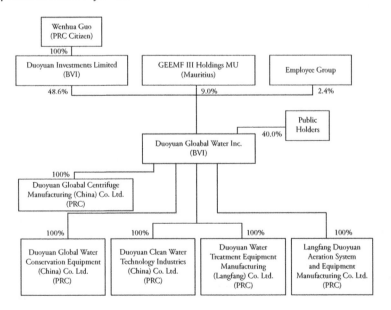

Case Study 5.3: Winsway Coking Coal Holdings

Background

- Winsway (SEHK ticker 1733) is an integrated supplier of coking coal to China. In addition, it provides services such as coal-processing plants and road and railway transportation capabilities. The company is headquartered in Hong Kong and has its main operations in Mongolia.
- The company is registered in the BVI, and is the holding company for Winsway Coking Coal Holdings (HK), which in turn has a 100 percent ownership of Cheer Top (BVI). This entity thus holds 100 percent of the onshore operating assets in Beijing Winsway (PRC) and Inner Mongolia Haotong (PRC).

Corporate Structure

- Winsway was listed on the Hong Kong stock exchange in October 2010. The IPO was underwritten by Merrill Lynch, Goldman Sachs, and Deutsche Bank. The company raised $560 million.
- The company issued a U.S. dollar high-yield bond in April 2011. The terms of the issue were: US$500 million, five-year tenor, 8.5 percent coupon, senior unsecured, callable in April 2014 at par.
- The company has a market capitalization of $670 million, debt of around $582 million, and $400 million in cash.
- Operating metrics were looking healthy, with reported revenues of $1.8 billion and earnings before interest, taxes, depreciation, and amortization (EBITDA) of $290 million. Ratios looked reasonable, with EV/EBITDA 3×, total debt/EBITDA 2×, EBITDA/interest 7.5×.
- Winsway had access to $800 million of credit facilities from both offshore and onshore banks. Offshore banks were OCBC, ABC, DB, ING, ANZ, Rabobank, ING. Onshore banks were Everbright and Bank of Nanjing. A third of their cash on hand ($130 million) is onshore.
- Chairman Wang owned 48 percent of the company, with Peabody Energy holding a strategic 5 percent stake. Mr. Delbert Lobb of Peabody was on the board of directors.
- KPMG is the auditor.

What Happened

- On 19 January 2011, Jonestown Research published a report accusing Winsway of fraud on two counts:
  1. Overstating their coal inventory by HKD 1 billion in 2011.
  2. Engaging in undisclosed related-party transactions with the coal transport companies in Mongolia.

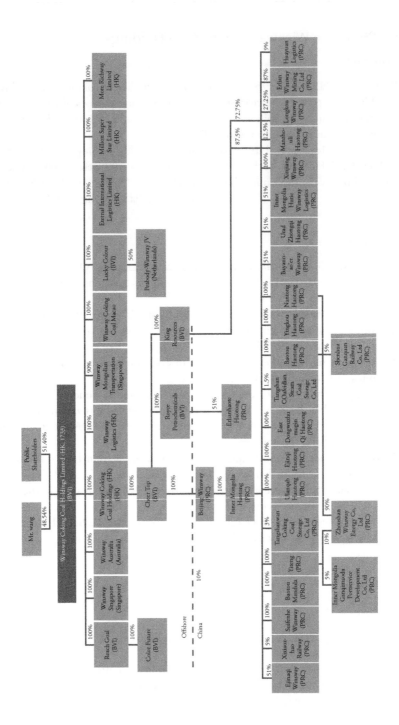

- The Jonestown research alleged that looking through the balance sheet from the IPO prospectus, and reconciling the amount of coal bought and sold, the inventory on the balance sheet is overstated.

Step 1: Calculate 2007 Beginning Tons of Inventory on the Balance Sheet

	31/12/2007
A. Ending Raw Coal Value (RMB) per p. I-49	169,040,000
Cos(RMB)/Ton per p. 223	284
Ending Raw Coal (Tons)	595,211
B. RMB Increase in Inventories from Cash Flow Statement (p. I-15)	143,388,000
Cos(RMB)/Ton per p.223	284
Net Increase in Raw Coal Inventories (Tons)	504,887
C. Ending Raw Coal (Tons)	595,211
−Net Increase in Raw Coal Inventories (Tons)	504,887
2007 Beginning Raw Coal Inventory (Tons)	**90,324**

Step 2: Reconcile Inventory Tonnage from 1/1/2007–30/6/2010

	31/12/2007	31/12/2008	31/12/2009	30/6/2010
A. Cleaned Coal Sold (Tons) per p. 222	—	657,895	1,796,081	1,551,157
Adjust to Raw Coal Equivalent at 75% Wash Rate	—	**877,193**	**2,394,775**	**2,068,209**
B. Raw Coal Sold (Tons) per p. 222	539,789	350,260	344,811	697,070
Raw Coal and Raw Coal Equivalent Sold (Tons)	**539,789**	**1,227,453**	**2,739,586**	**2,765,279**
C. Beginning Raw Coal and Equivalents Balance (Tons)	90,324	515,529	556,066	1,588,116
−Raw Coal Purchases (Tons) per p. 223	964,994	1,267,990	3,771,636	2,366,763
−Raw Coal Sold (Tons, Including Equivalent Amount)	539,789	1,227,453	2,739,586	2,765,279
Ending Raw Cool and Equivalents Balance (Tons)	**515,529**	**556,066**	**1,588,116**	**1,189,600**
D. Beginning Hard Coal Balance (Tons)	—	—	—	428,291
−Hard Coal Purchases (Tons) per p. 223	—	—	3,361,228	1,995,687
−Hard Coal Sold (Tons) per p. 222	—	—	2,932,937	2,007,233
Ending Hard Coal Balance (Tons)	—	—	**428,291**	**416,745**

Step 3: Calculate the Ending Tons of from the Balance Sheet

	31/12/2007	31/12/2008	31/12/2009	30/6/2010
A. Ending Value Raw (RMB) per p. I-49	169,040,000	170,120,000	487,049,000	460,299,000
COS (RMB/Ton) Raw per p. 223	284	407	401	327
Ending Balance (Tons) Raw	**595,211**	**417,985**	**1,214,586**	**1,407,642**
B. Ending Value Cleaned (RMP)				
per p. I-49	—	117,613,000	222,092,000	237,653,000
COS (RMB/Ton) Raw per p. 223	—	614	631	654
COS (RMB/Ton) Raw Equivalent for				
Cleaned-@ 75% Wash Rate	—	461	473	491
Ending Balance (Tons) Raw				
Equivalent	—	**255,403**	**469,291**	**484,512**
C. Ending Value Hard (RMB) per p. I-49	—	—	285,018,000	290,414,000
COS (RMB/Ton) Hard per p. 223	—	—	846	1,047
Ending Balance (Tons) Hard	—	—	**336,901**	**277,377**

- This is an easy way for the company to report higher revenues and hide the lack of cash from higher earnings by claiming that it had been spent on inventory.
- The other allegation is that the transport of Mongolian coal into China via Moveday and Sanhe were undisclosed related-party transactions. Sanhe was previously a subsidiary of Winsway, but was reported to be divested to independent third parties in the IPO prospectus. The Jonestown report cites sources that the person Sanhe was sold to, Mr. Sun Hongzhou, is actually a related party due to his positions in Urad Zhongqi Yiten Mining (direct subsidiary of Winsway), and Tianjin Winsway Chemical Storage (related company owned by Chairman Wang). Thus, this is an undisclosed related-party transaction.
- Moveday is owned by Ng Pui Heng, who is reported to be working for Macau Winsway International Petrochemical Co. Ltd. (owned by Chairman Wang). The operating subsidiaries of Moveday are owned by a Singapore entity called Perfect Crown Pte Ltd., which is 10 percent owned by Mr. Ng.
- Moody's downgraded Winway's debt in May 2013 and warned of a liquidity crunch in September 2013. Its stock price declined about 70 percent and in October 2013 the company offered to buy back debt at about one-third of face value claiming that this "is expected to provide a better recovery rate for the holders than in liquidation" (Bloomberg 2013).

Warning Signs

- Promoter of the company has multiple business interests but has decided to list only the least exciting businesses, keeping it at less than 50 percent stake. This can be a red flag for a lack of alignment of interests between management and the shareholders.

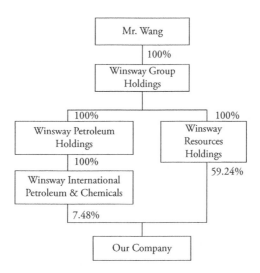

As can be seen from the preceding chart, Mr. Wang has other interests in the petrochemical industry.

- Related-party transactions—Moveday and Sanhe are both seemingly linked to Winsway. Control over the distribution network or in this case the transportation supplier will make it extremely easy for Winsway to move cash out of the company without auditors finding out. Moveday accounts for 41 percent of Winsway's coal procurement costs and has been paid $130 million over two years to transport the majority of Winsway coal from Mongolia to China. Furthermore, the lack of disclosure about these related parties does no favors for the level of corporate governance in Winsway.
- The business model is not transparent. Winsway buys coal from a supplier in Mongolia, then sells it to an import agent who takes delivery in Mongolia. The import agent moves the coal across the border to China, after which Winsway again buys the coal off the import agent and resells it to its end customer. This series of opaque and convoluted transactions, while disclosed, is a red flag, as it is very easy to falsify transactions.

Key Lessons

- Winsway has denied all allegations made by Jonestown. The CFO refuted the allegations of overstating inventory by saying that the starting and ending balances used to calculate the inventory are inaccurate as the inventory turnover is 2.5 months. Winsway also continues to maintain that the relationships between the company and Moveday and Sanhe are arm's-length transactions to independent parties.

- While the company has not been able offer irrefutable evidence against the Jonestown allegations, it is highly unlikely that the company is a fraud.
- KPMG signed off on the fiscal year 2011 audited financials on 26 March 2012. Given that the Jonestown report appeared before the annual report was published, KPMG would have been extra careful with its audit. The company has even declared a dividend for 2011, showing that the cash is real.
- Winsway completed the $1 billion acquisition of Canadian coal miner Grand Coal with Marubeni Corporation, a major Japanese commodities trader. They acquired the company via a 60:40 joint venture. Marubeni would not have proceeded with this deal had Winsway been unable to uphold its end of the bargain.
- Finally, state-owned CHALCO is buying a 29.9 percent stake in Winsway for $308 million from Chairman Wang. Chairman Wang will step down as chairman after the stake sale is completed, as he will no longer be a majority shareholder. As a state-owned enterprise, CHALCO's becoming the majority owner is a big boost for the credit rating of the company and has ended a lot of the speculation surrounding the company.
- While Winsway is unlikely to be a fraud, the lack of transparency surrounding the company's business practices has impacted investors. Winsway has gone from a high of HKD 2.50/share to HKD 1.33/share, representing a 47 percent fall in value, and the bonds traded down 10 percent after the allegations surfaced (although the bonds have rebounded since the CHALCO takeover).
- The key takeaways are that alignment of interest of the promoter (in this case we see that ultimately he was not interested in the business), the lack of transparency, and the questions about the related-party transactions all impact the share price and bond price of a company, even if it is not a fraud.

REFERENCES

Jonestown Research. 2011. Report on Winsway Coking Coal Holdings, January 19.
Muddy Waters Research. 2011. Report on Duoyuan Global Water, April 4.
Renhe Commercial Holdings. Annual Reports 2010 and 2011.
Ripley Capital. 2012. Report on Renhe Commercial Holdings, February 21.
Winsway Coking Coal Holdings. 2010. Initial Public Offering Prospectus and Annual Report.
Wong, Kelvin. 2013. "Renhe Credit Rating Cut by S&P as Developer May Face Cash Crunch," *Bloomberg*, April 5.
Yun, Michelle, and Rachel Evans. 2013. "Winsway Buys Back Debt After Investors Agree Sweetened Bond Deal." Bloomberg, October 9.

CHAPTER 6

EVALUATING CORPORATE GOVERNANCE AND RELATED-PARTY ISSUES

This chapter examines the impact of weak corporate governance on reported results. Weak corporate governance provides opportunities for the activities presented in previous chapters by permitting managers or majority shareholders to engage in related-party transactions to enrich themselves at the expense of other shareholders. The chapter provides a checklist of things to look for when evaluating corporate governance issues.

When an investor is also the manager, there is an automatic alignment of interests. The owner would run the business in its best interests and would be disincentivized to enter into transactions that detract from this mission. In today's large public companies, this alignment is harder to achieve due to a separation of ownership and control. The investors provide capital to the business, which is in turn run by its management. With the investor base being very fragmented, no single investor is able to exercise oversight to ensure that the owners' interests are looked after. Good corporate governance can overcome the issues associated with a separation of ownership and control.

137

According to the CFA Institute:

> Corporate governance is the system of internal controls and procedures by which individual companies are managed. It provides a framework that defines the rights, roles, and responsibilities of various groups—management, board, controlling shareowners, and minority or non-controlling shareowners—within an organization.
>
> At its core, corporate governance is the arrangement of checks, balances, and incentives that a company needs in order to minimize and manage the conflicting interests between insiders and external shareowners. Its purpose is to prevent one group from expropriating the cash flows and assets of one or more other groups.

Good corporate governance includes a strong independent board of directors, strong internal and external audit functions, transparent disclosures, incentives for management to act in the best interest of shareholders and strong shareowner rights. If corporate governance is not strong, management or the board may engage in transactions that are not in the best interests of investors. These can include related-party transactions, personal use of company assets, expropriation of assets, excessive compensation, and decisions that keep management entrenched.

BOARD GOVERNANCE AND INDEPENDENT DIRECTORS

As noted in the introduction to this chapter, good corporate governance includes a strong independent board of directors. It is desirable for a majority of the board to be independent nonexecutive directors. Additionally, the directors should not have other business interests related to the company or its auditors. An independent board can reduce the possibility of inappropriate related-party transactions or similar activities. Interestingly, in the Sino-Forest case discussed earlier, the audit committee of the board had two independent directors (out of four members of the audit committee) that were former partners of the company's audit firm. This is a red flag, as these "independent" directors may not use the necessary amount of professional skepticism in overseeing company activities and the audit process.

A recent study by the CFA Institute of 1,184 companies traded on the Hong Kong Stock Exchange showed that while 77 percent of the companies had independent directors comprising at least one-third of their boards, only 9.3 percent had a majority of independent directors. We suggest that you prefer at least 50 percent of the board be independent nonexecutive directors, failing which extra diligence should be afforded when analyzing the company.

Weak corporate governance also exists if the CEO concurrently holds the position of chairman of the board without independent audit, nomination, and compensation committees made up primarily of independent nonexecutive directors.

The following are further evidence of strong corporate governance:

- Minority shareholder involvement in the nomination process.
- Formal director training and qualifications.
- Directors are not past employees, members of professional firms doing work for the company or have had a business relationship with the company other than serving as a director.

SHAREOWNER RIGHTS

Owning shares of a business enterprise is a necessary but insufficient condition for an investment to have value. Not all shares are created equal, and the rights associated with publicly held shares are a critical aspect of their value. Often, particularly among companies in Asia, there are different rights associated with different share classes, which diminish the value of some shares relative to others and enable some shareholders to benefit themselves more than others. The CFA Institute has recommended the following considerations in evaluating shareowner rights:

- Are there different classes of shares, and how do voting rights differ between them?
- Does the company have safeguards in its articles of organization or by-laws that protect the rights and interests of those shareowners whose shares have inferior rights?
- Was the company recently privatized by a government or government entity and if so, whether the selling government has retained voting rights that could veto certain decisions of management and the board? Further, can a government prevent shareowners from receiving full value for their shares?
- Have the super voting rights granted to certain classes of shareowners impaired the company's ability to raise equity capital for future investment?
- Are shareholders able to vote their shares by proxy if they are unable to attend a shareowners' meeting, and have they been afforded sufficient time to review and analyze information in advance of the meeting?
- Are shareowners able to cast confidential votes?
- Are shareowners able to cast the cumulative number of votes allotted to their shares for one or a limited number of board nominees?
- Do shareowners have the right to approve changes to corporate structures and policies that may alter the relationship between shareowners and the company?
- May shareowners submit proposals for consideration at the company's annual meeting, and is management required to implement any approved proposals?[1]

INTERLOCKING OWNERSHIP OR DIRECTORSHIPS

The opportunity for managers or some shareholders to benefit from dealings with the company at the expense of other shareholders is increased when there are interlocking ownership structures or interlocking directorships. In particular, these situations often lead to related-party transactions (discussed in the next section), and they are quite common in some countries in Asia (*keiretsu* and *chaebol*).

In an interlocking ownership structure, there are many firms that each own shares in each other. While this can insulate the group from takeovers, it puts individual shareholders of the individual companies at a disadvantage. Similar situations occur when there are multiple companies where they share directors or where management of Company A serves as a director of Company B, and management at Company B serves on the board of Company A.

You should examine the ownership and director structure of a company to determine if there are interlocking directorship or ownership situations and, if so, be more skeptical and perform more due diligence. The more complex the ownership structure, the more work needs to be done.

RELATED-PARTY TRANSACTIONS

A related-party transaction involves the company's engaging in a transaction with a member of management, board member, a member of management's family, or the board or another entity controlled by one of these related parties (or when there are interlocking ownership or directorship situations). The transaction could be a business transaction involving revenue or an expense of the company, a purchase or sale of an asset from a related party, a lease of an asset from or to a related party, or a borrowing transaction. Such transactions may occur if their terms are the same as those that would have been used in an arm's-length transaction with an unrelated party; however, they need to be disclosed so that investors can judge their appropriateness. Analysts should scrutinize these transactions carefully when disclosed and perform due diligence to identify potential undisclosed related-party transactions.

The 2010 annual report of Sino-Forest (case discussed in more detail in Chapter 2) disclosed a series of related-party transactions with regard to Greenheart Group and executives of Sino-Forest. Footnotes 25 and 26 of that report stated (amounts in USD):

> 25. Related Party Transactions
>
> [a] Pursuant to the respective service agreements, the Company pays the salaries of certain executive officers in the form of consultancy fees to companies controlled by the executive officers. The consultancy fees

incurred for the year amounted to $8,242,000 [2009—$7,569,000] and were recorded at an exchange amount as agreed by the related parties.

[b] In addition, as at December 31, 2010, $7,632,000 [2009—$6,958,000] was accrued for consultancy fees payable to these related companies. The amount was included in accounts payable and accrued liabilities in the financial statements.

[c] On February 6, 2009, the Company entered into an agreement to acquire 55,000,000 ordinary shares and approximately $21,706,000 (equivalent to approximately HKD 167,631,000) 4% secured convertible bonds of Greenheart Group from various vendors. Total consideration was approximately $25,775,000 (equivalent to approximately HKD 200,631,000). Among the vendors was a director of the Company and an entity controlled by such director, the aggregate value of whose Greenheart Group ordinary shares and convertible bonds represented approximately 5.5% of the aggregate value of the overall transaction.

[d] In June 2010, the Company acquired 2,638,469,000 ordinary shares of Greenheart Resources. Total consideration was approximately $33 million. One of the vendors, Forest Operations Limited, which is beneficially owned by a director of the Company, owned approximately 5.3% of the ordinary shares sold.

[e] On August 17, 2010, Greenheart Group issued an aggregate principal amount of $25,000,000 2015 Greenheart Group Convertible Notes for gross proceeds of $24,750,000. The sole subscriber to the 2015 Greenheart Group Convertible Notes is a company in which a director of the Company has an indirect interest.

26. Subsequent Event

On January 7, 2011, the Company entered into a sales and purchase agreement to dispose of the Mangakahia Forest a radiate pine plantation in New Zealand to Greenheart Group for a consideration of approximately $71 million, subject to adjustments upon the completion of the sale. The consideration will be settled partly in cash and partly in the form of shares of Greenheart Group.

Note that it is unusual for compensation of executives to be paid through another company as consulting fees, and in this case, it appears the payments were accrued and not paid, which could indicate a lack of cash in Sino-Forest to pay the fees. The remaining transactions related to the acquisition of Greenheart, involving a director of Sino-Forest. This might indicate that the company did not reach an arm's-length price and that this director benefitted at the expense of Sino-forest shareowners. More interesting is the Ontario Securities Commission's finding that the chairman and CEO of Sino-Forest controlled two holding companies that owned interests in Greenheart and that he received $22 million as a result of the purchase by Sino-Forest.

Application: PUDA Coal

PUDA Coal was a New York Stock Exchange (NYSE)–listed company that was accused by a forensic accounting firm of engaging in transactions to expropriate company assets for the benefit of the chairman of the company. They engaged in a variety of other related-party transactions. PUDA owed Chairman Zhao a principal amount of RMB240M (US$36.4 million) based on a loan agreement dated 7 May 2010. The loan proceeds were used to increase Shanxi Coal's registered capital to the level required by the Shanxi government to be a coal mine consolidator. Chairman Zhao could cause PUDA to default on the loan agreement of 7 May 2010, as he would be entitled to an additional 5 percent penalty interest on top of the 6 percent regular interest under the loan. This provided a win-win situation for him regardless of the outcome.

In addition, Yao Zhao (brother of the chairman) is a 75 percent owner of Shanxi LiulinJucai Coal Industry Co. Ltd, which supplies raw coal to Shanxi Coal (90 percent subsidiary of PUDA). Yao Zhao was appointed as chief operating officer (COO) of Shanxi Coal and manager of its coal-washing plants in 1999, and COO of PUDA from July 2005 to November 2006.

Chairman Zhao owned Resources Group, in addition to controlling the six mines under the Pinglu Project, where PUDA received most of its coal. The Zhaos could impact PUDA's production and revenue by limiting PUDA's coal supply, and cause PUDA to default on its loans to Resources Group. In such a case, Resources Group could acquire PUDA's assets—and, ultimately, both the Zhaos would own the assets.

EXCESSIVE COMPENSATION

Management may enrich themselves at the expense of shareholders by compensating themselves in excess of the amount warranted for the job and their performance. This can occur even when management owns a significant percentage of the company. For example, if management owns 30 percent of the company but takes out 1 million Hong Kong dollars in excess compensation, the majority of the cost (70 percent) is borne by the other owners. Companies should fully disclose the nature of compensation including specifics on the terms of any bonus or stock option packages so that analysts can evaluate the level of compensation relative to peer companies as well as any incentives the plan creates to manipulate financial results.

PERSONAL USE OR EXPROPRIATION OF ASSETS

Management or others in the company may convert assets to personal use or for personal benefit. This can range from the personal use of a company's airplane to the embezzlement of company assets, including cash. Related-party transactions, complex structures, and complex transactions are often used to expropriate assets at a low price to the related buyer. Embezzlement is a special case of expropriation of assets involving cash. In this case, the cash is taken out of the company and transactions are disguised as other business transactions, such as payment of business expenses or the purchase of inventory or equipment. However, the personal use or expropriation of assets is more likely to occur when there is weak corporate governance.

LACK OF TRANSPARENCY

As we have seen in the previous chapters, financial statements by themselves often do not show a full and complete picture of the underlying economic condition of a company. The footnotes, press releases, and other communications contain important disclosures that help the analyst understand the financial data better. Companies that are transparent and offer high-quality disclosures are also those that you can likely trust to avoid the types of accounting games you need to avoid. Poor-quality disclosures, however, often accompany these same accounting games. If a company does not disclose details to explain major transactions or uses limited language that obscures the underlying economics, you will need to work harder to evaluate the company.

AUDITOR ISSUES

External auditors perform an important function. They review the company's financial reports including footnotes and express an opinion regarding how the financial condition and performance of the company is reflected in the financial reports. It is essential that the auditors be independent of the company and management. If they are not independent, then their opinion cannot be relied upon. However, even with independent auditors there is no guarantee that the auditors will detect all the problems that may exist. So a clean audit opinion is not sufficient—in fact, for all of the cases in this book there was an "independent" external audit firm. Some were just not as independent and objective as they could have been.

At times, audit staff will be hired by the company to be a part of management or as a director. This results in the remaining auditors auditing the work of their former colleagues and perhaps supervisors, consequently creating an environment where the auditors' objectivity is put into question. Similarly, if the same audit firm and audit staff have been auditing the firm for many years, they may have gotten too comfortable with management and not be entirely objective. Therefore, you should be wary in these situations.

While some auditor rotation is desirable, you also need to be careful with the other extreme. If a company has frequently changed auditors (regardless if it was management's idea or the auditors resigning on their own accord), it may be a sign of underlying problems. You should be particularly careful when auditors resign or report disagreements with management. Further, you should look for the auditors' opinion not just on the financial statements but on the company's internal control systems. Lack of strong internal controls provides opportunities for accounting manipulation.

The work of the auditors should be overseen by an audit committee ideally composed entirely of independent nonexecutive directors to which the internal audit staff of the company should report.

While rare, you should also be wary of situations where the audit firm is small and does not have the resources to properly audit a public company. Be particularly careful if the auditor has had audit failures at other companies.

Application: China Valves Tech

The full case is detailed at the end of this chapter. The company was recently challenged regarding a number of accounting issues. The company's auditor, Frazer Frost, was a smaller accounting firm that audited a number of Chinese companies where scandals occurred (the company has since split up).

PARTING COMMENTS

Corporate governance is a key factor in the ability of management to play accounting games and go undetected. You should evaluate the company's corporate governance level and invest an inversely proportionate amount of your time with other forms of analysis: if corporate governance is weak you will need to increase your analysis and due diligence dramatically—or avoid an investment in the company altogether. Exhibit 6.1 provides a checklist of factors to consider with regard to corporate governance.

EXHIBIT 6.1   Checklist of Warning Signs and Analysis Techniques

Board Governance and Independence	• Examine board membership for external members. Corporate governance is weak for boards comprised of less than 50 percent independent non-executive directors. • Be wary when the CEO also serves as chairman of the board of directors. • Are there separate board audit, nomination, and compensation committees comprised primarily of independent directors? If not, exercise more due diligence. • Examine possible interlocking directors.
Shareowner Rights	• Are there different classes of shares, and how do voting rights differ between them? If so, are there safeguards in its articles of organization or bylaws that protect the rights and interests of those shareowners whose shares have inferior rights? • Was the company recently privatized by a government or government entity with retained voting rights that could veto certain decisions of management and the board? • Are shareholders able to vote their shares by proxy if they are unable to attend a shareowners' meeting, cast confidential votes, submit matters to a vote, and approve changes to corporate structure and policies?
Interlocking Ownership or Directorships	• Are their interlocking ownership or directorship arrangements? If so, increase analysis and due diligence.
Related-Party Issues	• Are there business transactions between company and management? • Are family members of management involved in the company or other companies with which the subject company does business? • Are there significant loans to management or affiliated companies either from the company or related entities?
Excessive Compensation and Personal Use of Assets	• Are there sufficient and clear disclosures of compensation or perks of management so that they can be evaluated with reference to similar companies? • Are there sufficient internal controls to prevent personal use or expropriation of corporate assets? • Is there excessive use of stock-based compensation/options?
Lack of Transparency	• Does the company resist making detailed disclosures or use language that obscures what is going on?
Auditor Issues	• Are auditors truly independent and objective? Are there any conditions that may impair their objectivity? Is the audit firm large enough and possessing a sufficiently high-quality reputation to audit a public company? • Have there been resignations of, frequent changes in, or disagreements with auditors? • Is there a strong independent audit committee of the board and strong internal controls to mitigate other issues?

CASE STUDIES

The following cases examine companies that may have been accused—but not necessarily ascertained guilty—of manipulating their reported results. These cases demonstrate many of the concepts presented in this chapter. Note that some concepts in these cases may be related to concepts covered in other chapters; however the full case is included for completeness and to demonstrate that there is often a plural nature of accounting manipulation.

Case Study 6.1: China Valves Tech (Nasdaq: CVVT)

Background

- China Valves Technology (CVVT) is a developer, manufacturer, and after-market service provider of comprehensive flow management products and services in China. The company's valves are used in different industrial applications, including nuclear power, fossil power, hydropower, oil and gas, and so on.
- The company was formed in 2007 with the merger of two leading fluid motion and control companies: ZD Valves and Kaifeng Valves. CVVT has six wholly owned subsidiaries: Zhengzhou City ZD Valves Co. Ltd., Henan Kaifeng High Pressure Valves Co. Ltd., TaizhouTaideValves Co. Ltd., Yangzhou Rock Valves Lock Technology Co. Ltd., China Valves Technology (Changsha) Valves Co. Ltd., and Shanghai PudongHanweiValve Co. Ltd.
- CVVT completed three major acquisitions in 2009 and 2010: Able Delight, Hanwei Valves, and Yangzhou Rock.
- CVVT has been growing predominantly through acquisitions, including the recent purchase of Yangzhou Rock Valves Lock Technology. Although these purchases are accretive to earnings, Yangzhou's product line has so far resulted in considerably lower margins as rising raw material costs coupled with significantly lower-priced product sales eat into margins.
- In its most recent filing, China Valves reported gross margins of 45.4 percent in the third quarter of 2010 compared to 49.3 percent in the same period previous year.
- Auditor: Frazer Frost.

What Happened

- In January 2011, Citron Research put out a research alerting investors of potential areas of misrepresentation and nondisclosure in the company's 8-K reports filed to the SEC, in the area of CVVT's three acquisitions.
- Able Delight: US$15 million acquisition:

On 12 January 2010, CVVT announced its intention to acquire assets of Able Delight for US$15 million, a few weeks after closing a US$22 million private placement. The transaction was completed 3 February 2010. In CVVT's February 8-K filed, the assets purchased included US$4.9 million of inventory and US$10.1 million of property, plant, and equipment (PP&E).

In November 2010, CVVT amended the 8-K and disclosed for the first time that Able Delight was a subsidiary of Watts Water Tech (NYSE: WTS). Securities and Exchange Commission (SEC) 10-Q and 10-K filings from WTS showed that Able Delight (Changsha) Valves lost US$5.3 million in 2009 and was under an investigation on foreign corrupt practices. WTS shut it down as a result of that.

However, CVVT estimated for FY2010, Able Delight would contribute US$20.5 million in revenue (twice the previous revenue by WTS), and US$5 million net income.

In the amended November 8-K filed, it was revealed that only US$6.1 million was paid for "assets" of Able Delight to WTS (WTS filed that they received US$5 million), and an additional US$8.9 million went to Able Delight's owner, Qing Lu, as a loan. Qing Lu shares the same residential address and co-owns the same house as Bin Li (34 percent owner of CVVT and first cousin of Siping Fang, chairman of CVVT).

- HanweiValve:

    CVVT's acquisition of HanweiValve also saw a different 8-K on its 9 April 2010, filings.

    The "Asset Transfer Agreement" referenced in the 8-K contained four parties as follows:

    A. Henan Tonghai Fluid Equipment Co. Ltd. (subsidiary of CVVT).
    B. Shanghai PudongHanweiValve Co. Ltd. (acquired company).
    C. Shanghai HanhuangValves Co. Ltd. (owner of B).
    D. Hong Kong Hanxi Investment Co. Ltd. (owner of B).

    In CVVT's 8-K, it was stated that parties C and D, which owned Shanghai PudongHanweiValve, are unrelated parties.

    However, Citron uncovered a document showing that China Valves owned party C prior to the acquisition. This meant that the acquisition of HanweiValve was in fact an undisclosed related-party transaction.

    Moreover, CVVT claims that this transaction is an "asset sale," and parties C and D represent that the tangible and intangible assets of HanweiValve (including but not limited to land, buildings, equipment, and intellectual property) are not subject to any collateral, pledge, lien, or any third-party claims. Parties C and D will assume all responsibilities arising out of any claims if the representations are inaccurate. It further lays on noncompete clauses.

In reality, CVVT did not buy just the assets, but the whole company (which could easily include undisclosed liabilities).

- Yangzhou Rock: US$7.3 million acquisition:

    CVVT paid US$6 million up front for Yangzhou Rock even before both parties agreed on the final price for the transaction.

    The price that CVVT paid for Yangzhou Rock was at a very low 2.2× price-to-earnings (P/E) ratio.

    Through CVVT's own filings and disclosure on the above three acquisitions, the company claimed an annualized revenue of US$94 million and blended gross margin of 43.4 percent on the acquisitions—quite optimistic!

    The stock that one time traded at $16 per share (2009) saw its price decline from about $10 per share in early 2011 to less than $1 per share in 2013.

Warning Signs

- CVVT had one of the lowest corporate governance scores (ranked 63rd out of 70 companies) on a recent Piper Jaffrey China investment study.
- The company has had a revolving door of chief financial officers (CFOs).
- The company's auditor, Frazer Frost, was a smaller accounting firm that audited a number of Chinese companies where scandals occurred (the company has since split up).
- Nothing about the company seems to make sense:
  - Their gross margins are the highest in a commoditized sector, yet they make no investments for innovation (their research-and-development budget for 2010 was around $150,000).
  - They compare themselves to Emerson, a company 100 times larger, yet CVVT claims they have twice the operating margins.
  - They are able to buy a competitor (Yangzhou Rock) at a P/E of 2.2.

Key Lessons

- The case of CVVT seems to be a case where the company's management started by making extremely optimistic revenue projections, which inflated the company's stock price. Following this, they raised funds via a private placement and then drained the funds from the company through related-party transactions, namely, the acquisitions listed earlier.
- Investors should not simply take management's word when they announce their revenue projections, and it is important to make independent judgments about how realistic their revenue projections are.
- It is also important to do background checks on parties involved in major transactions to find out if there are in fact undisclosed related-party transactions.

Case Study 6.2: PUDA COAL (OTC: PUDA UV)

Background

- PUDA Coal is a Chinese coal-mining company (NYSE-listed) that supplies premium cleaned coking coal to steel manufacturers within Shanxi province. The industry that PUDA operated in was characterized by low margins and high volumes.
- The company is registered in the British Virgin Islands, and was listed through a reverse takeover in July 2005 on the NYSE. It had two public offerings in 2010: February 2010 for 3.28 million shares at $4.75 (net proceeds of approximately US$14.5 million), and December 2010 for 9 million shares at $12 (net proceeds approximately US$101.5 million). Fundraising was done through Macquarie Capital and Brean Murray.
- The company's sole revenue source was through its 90 percent indirect equity ownership in Shanxi Puda Coal Group Co. Ltd. (Shanxi Coal). Business was derived from two segments: coal washing and coal mining.
- The company had a market cap of US$494.1 million at its peak at $16.47 per share, with debt of US$37.7 million and cash of US$156.2 million.
- PUDA seemed to be a profitable, well-run company based on its balance sheet and operation statements.

    Cash held in fiscal year 2010 was US$156.1 million versus US$19.9 million in fiscal year 2009, with a decrease in long-term debt at US$5.2 million in fiscal year 2010 versus US$6.5 million in fiscal year 2009. Net revenue saw a 52 percent increase from US$214 million to US$324 million, with revenue cost stable, contributing to 127 percent increase in gross profit of US$41.1 million for fiscal year 2010.

- PUDA's auditor was Moore Stephens.
- Major shareholders of the company:
    - Ming Zhao (chairman): 25.3 percent
    - Yao Zhao (chairman's brother): 6.34 percent
    - Wizel Lawrence (former member of board of directors): 0.04 percent
    - Tang C Mark (former member of board of directors): 0.04 percent
    - Jianfel Ni (former member of board of directors): 0.04 percent

What Happened

- In April 2011, GeoInvesting and another research firm, Alfred Little, published their findings of possible fraudulent activities in PUDA.

    The SEC began investigations, and on 22 February 2012, publicly announced they were charging Chairman Ming Zhao and CEO Liping Zhu in the following areas:

- Defrauding investors into believing they were investing in a Chinese coal business, when it was in fact an empty shell company.
- Failure to disclose transfer of PUDA's 90 percent stake in Shanxi Coal to Chairman Zhao, and later selling 49 percent of that stake to CITIC Trust.
- Further fraud by Zhao and Zhu in forging a letter from CITIC.

Timeline of events unfolding:

- September 2009: Chairman Zhao transferred PUDA's 90 percent stake in Shanxi Coal to himself, which gave him ownership of Shanxi Coal. This happened without shareholders' knowledge and approval.
- July 2010: Zhao transferred 49 percent of "his" interest in Shanxi Coal to CITIC. CITIC placed this 49 percent stake in Shanxi Coal into CITIC Trust, and sold interests in that trust to Chinese investors.

Zhao also made Shanxi Coal pledge the remainder 51 percent of its assets to CITIC Trust, as collateral for a loan of RMB$3.5 billion (US$516 million) from the trust to Shanxi Coal. Zhao then used this loan to purchase 1.2 billion preferred shares in CITIC Trust.

This left PUDA as a shell company with no ongoing business operations.

- 2011: SEC begins investigations. Chairman Zhao and CEO Zhu continue to deceive investors. Zhu forged a letter from CITIC Trust, falsely stating that no funds were loaned to Shanxi Coal and disclaiming any interest in PUDA or Shanxi Coal's assets. CEO Zhao's counsel (Shearman and Sterling) provided the forged letter to the SEC's investigative staff and PUDA's audit committee. After PUDA disclosed the letter in an SEC filing and further misled shareholders about the ownership of PUDA's assets, CEO Zhu admitted forging the letter and resigned as CEO. In September 2011, Zhao's legal counsel, Shearman & Sterling, resigned as Zhao's legal counsel. Banking firms Brean Murray and Macquarie Capital, which underwrote PUDA's secondary offerings and had a price target of US$21, ceased coverage, citing a "lack of clarity in its corporate governance."
- May 2011: Chairman Zhao came out to state his willingness to buy out remaining shares of PUDA that he did not already own at up to $12 per share, provided he could find financing to do so. The offer was nonbinding and preliminary with no financing, timeline, or any degree of certainty in place. However, nothing came through on the financing end, and news of the potential buyout offer died down.
- August 2011: NYSE delisted PUDA, and issued an order suspending trading in PUDA through 1 September 2011. On 28 September 2011, PUDA's CFO resigned, and neither CEO Zhu nor the CFO has been replaced.

- February 2012: SEC filed a lawsuit against PUDA's Chairman and former CEO on grounds that both worked to secretly transfer PUDA's controlling interest in *Shanxi Coal* to Chairman Zhao, and failed to disclose to investors through its financial reports. The SEC further stated PUDA's two public offerings (in February 2010 and December 2010) to raise capital for mine acquisitions by Shanxi Coal were without proper representation, on the grounds that PUDA did not disclose that it no longer owned any ownership stake in Shanxi Coal since September 2009.
- March 2012: Three of the board members—Lawrence Wizel, C. Mark Tang, Jianfei Ni—resigned from the board and all the board committees that they served on in PUDA.
- April 2012: PUDA announced its board unanimously consented to the Audit Committee's decision to launch a full investigation into the allegations raised regarding the unauthorized transactions. The Audit Committee retained professionals in the United States and China to assist PUDA in its investigation, and the full board, including Chairman Ming Zhao, agreed to cooperate in the investigation.
- Ongoing: Investigations are still in preliminary stages, and there is supporting evidence of transfers by Chairman Zhao that were inconsistent with disclosures made by PUDA in its public securities filings. Zhao has agreed to a voluntary leave of absence as chairman of the board of PUDA until the investigations are completed.
- At present, PUDA is trading on the over-the-counter exchange in the United States at about $0.10 per share, with a market cap of US$3 million.

Warning Signs

- *Cash flow from investing.* In August 2010, Shanxi Coal entered into an investment cooperation agreement with Chairman Zhao and an unrelated individual, Jianping Gao. Both of them, together with Shanxi Coal, purchased the mining rights and assets of six coal mines in Pinglu County for US$53.4 million.

  The amount was largely financed by loans by the banks, and the money was held by Resources Group, a firm wholly owned by Chairman Zhao and his brother, Yao Zhao.
- *Related-party transactions.* PUDA owed Chairman Zhao a principal amount of RMB240 million (US$36.4 million) plus quarterly interest, based on a loan agreement dated 7 May 2010. The loan proceeds were used to increase Shanxi Coal's registered capital to the level required by the Shanxi government to be a coal mine consolidator.

  Chairman Zhao could cause PUDA to default on the loan agreement of 7 May 2010, as he would be entitled to an additional 5 percent penalty interest on top of the 6 percent regular interest under the loan. This provided a win-win situation for him regardless of the outcome.

In addition, Yao Zhao (brother of chairman) is a 75 percent owner of Shanxi LiulinJucai Coal Industry Co. Ltd., which supplies raw coal to Shanxi Coal (90 percent subsidiary of PUDA). Yao Zhao was appointed as COO of Shanxi Coal and manager of its coal-washing plants in 1999, and COO of PUDA from July 2005 to November 2006.

• *Conflict of interest.* Chairman Zhao owned Resources Group, in addition to controlling the six mines under the Pinglu Project, where PUDA received most of its coal.

The Zhaos could impact PUDA's production and revenue by limiting PUDA's coal supply, and cause PUDA to default on its loans to Resources Group. In such a case, Resources Group could acquire PUDA's assets—and, ultimately, both the Zhaos would own the assets.

• *Dividend payouts from Shanxi Coal not reaching shareholders in PUDA, and instead reaching Chairman Zhao and Yao Zhao.* In PUDA's 2010 annual report, it was mentioned that in 2005 Shanxi Coal (PUDA's 90 percent subsidiary) declared dividends of $1.72 million payable to Zhao (80 percent) and Yao Zhao (20 percent). In September 2008, Shanxi Coal declared an RMB$8 million (US$1.17 million) dividend to its shareholders, which was not paid as of 31 December 2010, the date of the 2010 annual report. No dividend was declared in 2009 or 2010, and PUDA stated the company did not intend to pay any dividends in the foreseeable future, as the board of directors intended to follow a policy of retaining earnings.

• *Resignation of auditor.* In July 2011, auditor Moore Stephens Hong Kong resigned, and stated further reliance should no longer be placed on its previously issued audit reports for PUDA's FY2009 and 2010. Moore Stephens stated PUDA had made representations to the audit reports that were "materially inconsistent" with the share transfers made by Chairman Zhao.

• *Publicly offering nonbinding announcement of a potential buyout.* When there was scrutiny from investors and the SEC on the financials, Chairman Zhao announced a nonbinding potential buyout offer. This gave the image of a firm that was worth its weight in its share price and could buy the company time to find a financier and direct investors' attention to the potential windfall of a buyout. This was similar to Harbin Electric, though in this case, PUDA was unsuccessful in finding a financier.

• *Corporate structure discrepancies.* PUDA employed an offshore ownership structure commonly used by public companies with operations in China. PUDA owned Puda Investment Holding Limited (Puda BVI), an international business company incorporated in the British Virgin Islands. Prior to the alleged violations (mentioned later), Puda BVI owned Shanxi Putai Resources Limited (Putai), a company established under the laws of China. PUDA's business operations were conducted exclusively through Shanxi Coal, which was 90 percent owned by Putai, 8 percent by Chairman Zhao, and 2 percent by Yao Zhao. PUDA had indirect ownership of the mining operations (Shanxi Coal) through a WFOE

(Putai), which directly owns 90 percent of the shares of Shanxi Coal. In the 10-K (16 March 2011), PUDA claimed the same corporate structure without reflecting the substantial changes.

Key Lessons

- *Alignment of interest between management and shareholders is of paramount importance.* Chairman Zhao knew his business and the regulatory risks in China better than PUDA's shareholders, and this gave him and his brother an advantage in outsmarting his shareholders. Chairman Zhao owned 100 percent of Resources Group but only 25.3 percent of PUDA Coal; this allowed him to focus on his personal gain of siphoning money from PUDA to Resources Group.
- *Close scrutiny of corporate governance is extremely important.* Chairman Zhao worked with his CEO Zhu to forge documents and hide the stake sale to CITIC Trust from shareholders. Understanding the background and history of the three men (Chairman Zhao; CEO Zhu; and the chairman's brother, Yao Zhao) and how they interlinked before setting up PUDA, would have yielded insights into the degree of corporate governance in the firm.
- *Natural resources in China are mostly held by state-owned enterprises and are interlinked to China's princelings (relatives of senior leaders).* Shanxi Coal was appointed by the Shanxi provincial government to consolidate nine thermal coal mines in Pinglu County, into five larger coal-mining operations. Asking the right questions to find out the persons involved in the deal would have given insight into how PUDA managed to get priority and the incentives given to the dealmakers.

Case Study 6.3: Sino-Environment Technology Group Limited

Background

- S-chip company based in Fujian that treats and manages industrial waste gas and industrial and municipal wastewater.
- Listed on the Mainboard of SGX on 28 April 2006. Genesis Capital Pte. Ltd. was the manager of SinoEnv's IPO, while SBI E2-Capital Asia Securities Pte. Ltd. was the co-manager, underwriter, and placement agent.
- Market capitalization of S$184.7 million on 31 December 2008, before chairman and CEO Sun Jiangrong defaulted on his S$120 million loan in March 2009.
- As of 31 December 2008, cash was 44.4 percent (S$147.1 million) of total assets (S$331.4 million). Net debt/equity was −0.13. Revenue was S$156.8 million, an increase of 67.3 percent year over year. However, the company made a net loss of S$9.1 million in FY2008, compared to a net profit of S$34.6 million in FY2007. This was largely due to fair value losses on the company's equity swap and embedded derivatives.

- Substantial shareholders as of 16 March 2009:
  - Chairman and CEO Sun Jiangrong: 51.23 percent.
  - DnB NOR Asset Management (Asia) Ltd.: 5.53 percent.
- Auditor: PricewaterhouseCoopers.

What Happened

2007

- Stark Investments, a global alternative investment firm, lent S$120 million to Thumb (China) Holdings (TCH), a private company wholly and beneficially owned by SinoEnv's chairman and CEO, Sun Jiangrong. TCH was also SinoEnv's controlling shareholder, with an ownership of 56.29 percent of SinoEnv's shares. As collateral for the S$120 million loan, Mr. Sun pledged his entire 56.29 percent shareholding in SinoEnv (190.8 million shares in the company). This security pledge was not disclosed in SinoEnv's 2007 annual report. Although TCH repaid S$55 million well before maturity, the remaining S$65 million came due on 16 February 2009, and TCH was unable to raise sufficient cash to repay Stark due to the global financial crisis. Moreover, talks between the parties failed because they were unable to reach an agreement on Stark's demand for additional collateral.
- Stark Investments is a hedge fund based in Wisconsin, founded in 1992 by Brian Stark and Mike Roth. In 2007, they were ranked the 31st-largest hedge fund in Institutional Investor's Hedge Fund 100. They held US$14.43 billion in assets under management as of 1 January 2008.

March 2009

- Sun Jiangrong defaulted on his S$120 million loan from Stark, on which he had pledged his full shareholding in SinoEnv (56.29 percent of the company).
- Stark enforced their security interests and forced the sale of his entire shareholding of SinoEnv in the open market. The loss of control of SinoEnv by Mr. Sun caused the company to default on its S$149 million convertible bond issue.

May 2009

- The board appointed NTan Corporate Advisory as the independent financial adviser to carry out a thorough and comprehensive review of the events that happened in March.
- PricewaterhouseCoopers (PwC) was engaged to perform a special audit on the company's cash transactions.
- Mass resignation of the China executive directors from their key management positions, but they were eventually reinstated.

September 2009

- Shares of the company were suspended from trading on the SGX on 24 September 2009.

October 2009

- Transactional risks: Special audit by PwC found that S$85 million of transactions were made by SinoEnv without board approval and authorization. Furthermore, no raw materials or equipment were delivered despite the purchase agreements, nor was there any significant work done at the projects that the group purportedly invested in.
  - One of SinoEnv's units, China Energy Environment, paid S$14 million to a Japanese firm (JGC Catalysts and Chemicals) for the purchase of raw materials, but JGC claimed that there was no such deal.
  - A SinoEnv unit, Fujian Fuda Desai Environmental Protection, invested S$50 million in four waste power plant projects, but no significant work had been carried out in August even though some construction was supposed to have been completed by April or May.
  - Installment payments of S$10 million made by unit Thumb Facilities to buy equipment for a plant.
  - Another group subsidiary Fujian Weidong EPT Co. made two interest-free loans totaling S$11 million to two parties not related to the group.
    Findings were reported to the Singapore and Chinese authorities, and the Independent Directions instructed the financial controller, Mr. Raynauld Liang, to assist the authorities with the investigation.

November 2009

- Financial Controller Mr. Liang's services were terminated on 10 November 2009, without board approval.
- Mr. Sun claimed that the company had cash holdings of S$40 million in a bank account in China. However, clarifications with the executive directors revealed that this was an estimated aggregate sum that included trade and other receivables, and the exact amount of cash reserves in the Xiamen bank was only S$14 million.

January 2010

- Fuzhou Public Security Bureau in China announced that it did not find any evidence to suggest that Mr. Sun had embezzled company funds and therefore was not placing the case on file.
- Mr. Sun resigned as chairman of SinoEnv, along with the firm's entire executive board.

March 2010

- Key management at the Fuzhou plant, led by Deputy General Manager Tian Yuan, who is the legal representative of Fujian Thumb Environment, a Sino-Environment subsidiary, pledged their support to restart business operations at SinoEnv in return for a stake of at least 20 percent through subscription of new shares.

September 2011

- AVIC International Investments, the shipbuilding management arm of the Aviation Industry Corp. of China Group, underwent an S-chip listing through a reverse merger with Sino-Environment on 12 September 2011.

Warning Signs

- *Alignment of the chairman's interests with the interests of the company.*
  - Chairman and CEO Sun Jiangrong owned 100 percent of TCH but only 56.29 percent of SinoEnv. There is a possibility that he will act in his own best interests rather than in the best interests of SinoEnv, especially after pledging his full shareholding in SinoEnv as collateral for his personal loan of S$120 million from Stark. This security pledge was not disclosed in SinoEnv's 2007 Annual Report, and this lack of transparency is an immediate red flag.
  - Stark was able to seize Mr Sun's entire stake in SinoEnv and sell it off in the open market in March 2009 soon after Mr. Sun defaulted on his loan. However, when Stark tried to win shares in Mr. Sun's RMB10 billion (S$2.02 billion) property developer, Chongqing Dading, to get further compensation, Mr. Sun tried various tactics to transfer the ownership of Chongqing Dading to an outside entity, allegedly controlled by his brother-in-law to prevent Stark from seizing the shares. Mr. Sun was also unwilling to provide Stark with additional collateral.
  - The relative ease with which Mr. Sun allowed Stark to seize SinoEnv's shares suggests it is highly likely that Mr. Sun's priorities lay with his other companies.

Key Lessons

- *Lack of transparency:* SinoEnv's annual reports do not contain any mention of Mr. Sun's pledge of his 56.29 percent stake in SinoEnv as collateral for his S$120 million loan.
- *Alignment of interest between executive directors and shareholders.* It appears that Mr. Sun's priorities did not lie with SinoEnv but with his other companies. The other executive directors also seemed to be more dedicated to the success of the company's subsidiaries back in China than to the success of ListCo in Singapore. During the May period, when they resigned temporarily from the board of SinoEnv, they continued to control and run the PRC subsidiaries.

• *Challenges in seeking redress for S-chips.* The probe conclusion by the Fuzhou Public Security Bureau claimed that it did not find any evidence to suggest that Chairman Sun had embezzled company funds when the evidence from PwC points to this, highlighting the challenges in seeking proper redress when it comes to S-chips.

NOTE

1. *The Corporate Governance of Listed Companies: A Manual for Investors,* 2nd ed. (Charlottesville, VA: CFA Institute, 2009), 29–35.

REFERENCES

Board Governance—How Independent Are Boards in Hong Kong Main Board Companies? 2012. Charlottesville, VA: CFA Institute.

Citron Research. 2012. "China Valve Technology—Destined to Get Delisted," June.

The Corporate Governance of Listed Companies: A Manual for Investors, 2nd ed. 2009. Charlottesville, VA: CFA Institute.

Geoinvesting LLC. 2011. Business Analysis Report on PUDA Coal, April 8.

Independent Non-Executive Directors: A Search for True Independence in Asia. 2010. Charlottesville, VA: CFA Institute.

Inter-Corporate Network Dealings and Minority Shareholder Protection—Cases in Japan. 2010. Charlottesville, VA: CFA Institute.

PUDA Coal Annual Reports, 2009 and 2010.

Related-Party Transactions: Cautionary Tales for Investors in Asia. 2009. Charlottesville, VA: CFA Institute.

SEC complaint dated February 2012. *Securities and Exchange Commission vs. Ming Zhao and Lipin Zhu.*

Shareowner Rights Across the Markets: A Manual for Investors. 2009. Charlottesville, VA: CFA Institute.

CHAPTER 7

SUMMARY AND GUIDANCE

This chapter pulls together the concepts presented in prior chapters and summarizes analysis techniques and warnings signs to look out for when evaluating the financial statements of Asian companies.

Accounting scandals have been around for as long as capital markets. Whenever you have a separation of ownership and control—where the individuals running a company are not the same as those providing the capital for its operations—there is an opportunity for the managers to obscure the true economic picture of what is going on in the business. Sometimes it starts innocently enough. Perhaps there has been a tough quarter and management makes some adjustments to avoid triggering the violation of a debt covenant, with the intent of reversing the manipulation in the subsequent period. However, if the economics do not improve in the subsequent period, the company may have to make bigger adjustments to continue to hide the prior manipulation, resulting in a snowball effect where the manipulations get increasingly larger over time. In other circumstances, the managers may have incentives, such as bonus arrangements, to make the reported results look better than reality. In more extreme cases, managers may have set out to commit fraud and loot as much as they can from the company and other shareholders.

These scandals have been global, such as the fraud of Ivar Kruger, the so-called Swedish match king, or the more recent cases of Parmalat in Italy or WorldCom in the United States. In recent years, it seems that more and more scandals have started to appear in the Asia Pacific region. This should not come as a surprise, as some of these capital markets are new or only recently opened to investors globally. As more investors seek to put capital to work in this region, the same incentives and opportunities that have existed in other capital markets arise. Further, as we noted in the Introduction, strong corporate governance has not yet taken hold in some of these markets. Investors need to be diligent in evaluating the possibilities for accounting games in all markets, being particularly cognizant where regulation and corporate governance practices are not yet fully developed.

In previous chapters, we presented an accounting framework and checklists of signs to look for in detecting different types of accounting games. In this chapter, we bring it all together to summarize the types of manipulations to look for, present a guide on how to approach the task of evaluating whether a company you are considering making an investment in may be engaged in such activities, and provide a master checklist of warning signs and analysis techniques. We also provide some additional cases from Asia Pacific companies so you can firm up your understanding with real-life examples.

PUTTING IT ALL TOGETHER

The previous chapters have shown that there are both quantitative and qualitative factors to consider when evaluating financial statements to determine whether they properly reflect economic reality. Quantitative factors are related to the nature of the articulation of financial statements. Qualitative factors include corporate governance and related issues, which can indicate whether there is a lack of control or oversight that can enable management or certain shareholders to enrich themselves at the expense of other shareholders.

The articulation of financial statements shows how the three main financial statements fit together: the income statement, the balance sheet and the cash flow statement. This is shown in Exhibit 7.1.

If management manipulates one financial statement, the impact is likely to be reflected on at least one other statement. The analyst is well advised to never focus on an individual financial statement but to study them collectively to look for imbalances or red flags.

The balance sheet is the core financial statement that connects the other two primary statements: the income statement and the statement of cash flows. Net income from the income statement is ultimately reflected in retained earnings on the balance sheet. Any increase in net income needs to be balanced by either an increase in assets, a decrease in liabilities, or a decrease in some other owners' equity account. Therefore, if managers want to manipulate net income, they must do so by also manipulating the balance sheet, creating warning signs that the analyst can observe. Similarly, the cash flow statement flows into the cash balance on the balance sheet. Any manipulation to overstate cash flows will result in an overstatement of cash on the balance sheet. While an overstatement of cash ought to be detected by auditors, there have been numerous cases in the Asia Pacific region in recent years where these

EXHIBIT 7.1   Articulation of Financial Statements

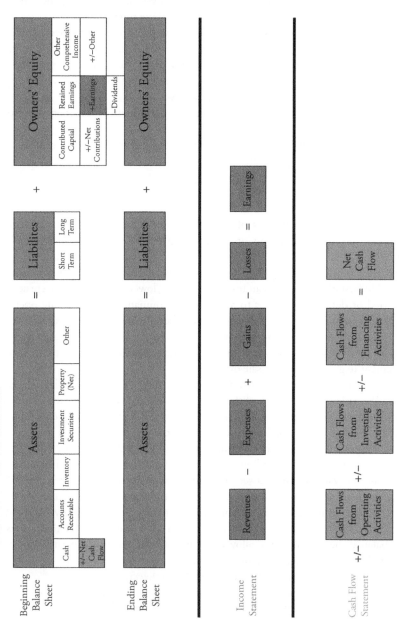

manipulations went undetected for some time. Eventually, however, these balance sheet bubbles must burst—the games cannot continue forever.

There are some manipulations that do not impact the balance sheet. The company might manipulate categories within the income statement or cash flow statement without overstating the bottom line on that statement. For example, they might overstate operating income without overstating net income or overstate operating cash flow without overstating net cash flow.

The most common manipulations impacting the financial statements include:

• Overstating earnings or misclassifying components of the income statement.
• Overstating financial position.
• Managing earnings.
• Overstating operating cash flow.

There are two main ways of overstating earnings on the income statement: aggressive revenue recognition or understating expenses. Aggressive revenue recognition might involve recording revenues too early, recording revenues for which collectability is doubtful, or, in the extreme case, recording revenues for fictitious sales. Understating expenses can involve reporting lower expenses than were actually incurred or deferring expenses to a later year. Companies may overstate operating earnings without overstating net income by either moving operating expenses to the non-operating section of the income statement (e.g., an "extraordinary or special charge") or by placing non-operating income in the operating section of the income statement (e.g., a gain on the sale of an asset).

There are several ways in which companies may overstate their financial position. The easiest way to accomplish this is to exclude an equal amount of assets and liabilities from the balance sheet maintaining the required balance. Their position is overstated, however, as the level of debt and income relative to assets is overstated. Companies may also focus just on manipulating the level of liabilities through off-balance-sheet financing or hiding losses off the financial statements. They may also overstate the value of some asset or resource, such as commodity reserves. These could be reflected on the balance sheet itself or reported in the footnotes.

Sometimes management is motivated to manage the variability or trend of earnings. In order to accomplish this, they must use accrual or deferral accounts on the balance sheet such as the allowance for doubtful accounts, unearned income, deferred taxes, contingencies, or reserves. These manipulations are typically less extreme than other games and are often harder to detect.

Cash flow manipulation most often involves an overstatement of operating cash flows (rather than investing or financing cash flows). Companies might engage in "real" activities that provide a temporary boost to cash flow such as acceleration of cash to be received or deferring cash to be paid. They may also engage in "artificial" means to overstate operating cash flows such as treating a borrowing transaction (a financing cash flow) as an operating cash flow or improperly classifying a normal expenditure as a capital expenditure (an investing cash flow).

Exhibit 7.2 presents a master checklist of warning signs and analysis techniques that you can use to examine the possibility that these games have been played on the financial statements.

On the qualitative side, you need to determine how comfortable you are with management and any other parties exerting control or influence over the company. These parties can take advantage of their position and the lack of controls at the company to benefit themselves at your expense. In the extreme, where there is a lack of strong corporate governance, auditor issues, and/or related-party transactions, you may just want to move on and find another investment. If governance and related-party issues exist to a lesser extent and you still want to consider an investment, you should perform extra due diligence, including looking for the warning signs previously listed. Exhibit 7.2 also provides techniques for analyzing the following qualitative issues:

- Board governance and independence.
- Shareowner rights.
- Interlocking ownership and directorships.
- Related-party issues.
- Excessive compensation and personal use of assets.
- Lack of transparency.
- Auditor issues.

A RECIPE FOR DETECTING COOKED BOOKS

While there is no one right way or specific order in which you should analyze a company to assess the possibility that they have engaged in accounting games, there are certainly some steps that should be part of the process. Before you start going through these steps, it is useful to re-read Exhibit 7.2 so the warnings signs and techniques will be fresh in your mind. Recommended steps include:

- *Understand the business.* You should thoroughly understand the business the company is in and identify the major peer companies so that you can use them as benchmarks. Understanding the business and peer companies will enable you to observe discrepancies on the financial statements—things that appear out of the ordinary for this type of company.
- *Gather and read through all of the financial statements and footnotes for the last several years.* This should include not just one set of financial statements that includes several years of financial statements but the separate reports for each of several years. You should read through these keeping in mind the checklist

EXHIBIT 7.2   Master Checklist of Warning Signs and Analysis Techniques

Overstated Earnings or Misclassified Components of the Income Statement

Aggressive revenue recognition	• Examine revenue recognition policy in footnotes relative to peers. • Are customer receivables growing faster than revenues? • Is operating cash flow significantly lower than accounting earnings? • Did significant revenues occur late in the year?
Understating/ Deferring expenses	• Are depreciation/amortization periods longer than those in peer companies? • Are there any deferred expenses listed as an asset on the balance sheet (other than deferred taxes)? • Are there any unusual assets or unexplained large increases in assets such as inventory, particularly relative to revenues?
Classification of non-operating income	• Were "gains" included in revenue? • Is the company's operating description appropriate? • Were one-time or nonrecurring items included in revenue? • Were any gains or revenue based on revaluation of assets?
Classification of operating expenses	• Were any expenses or losses listed as "special," extraordinary, or nonrecurring at the bottom of the income statement? • Are there unusually high margins relative to peers (also applies to deferral of expenses)?

Overstated Financial Position

Exclusion of assets and liabilities	• Is the company using operating leases to a greater extent than similar companies? • Is the company using the equity method of accounting for affiliates? How would the financials look if these affiliates were consolidated? • Has the company shifted accounts receivable off of the balance sheet in a transaction that would be better classified as borrowing? • Does the company have insufficient assets on its balance sheet to support reported operations and revenues, particularly relative to similar companies?
Off-balance-sheet liabilities/ financing	• Are there financing or guarantee arrangements disclosed in the footnotes of press articles that are not reflected on the balance sheet? • Are there discussions about contingencies or losses that are not currently reported on the income statement and for which no current liability is accrued?
Overstating assets	• Does the company have significant assets that are subject to estimates or assumptions, or where objective valuations are not available? • Does the company have unusual changes in the quantity or valuation of intangible assets, commodities, or biological assets (whether reported on the balance sheet or not)? • Were any gains or revenue based on revaluation of assets, and what percentage of their operating income comes from these activities?

EXHIBIT 7.2 *Continued*

Managed Earnings

Allowance for doubtful accounts	• Examine the allowance for doubtful accounts and bad debt expense relative to accounts receivable and revenue over time. Look for irregular patterns. • Examine the level of actual bad debts over time relative to the company's estimate in prior years.
Deferred or unearned income	• Look for accounts labeled deferred revenue or unearned revenue. • Consider whether advance collection is normal for this type of business. Does the deferral make sense? • Examine the balances from year to year to determine if their use increased or decreased revenue for the current year. • What would the company's revenue and profit have looked like without this deferral? Does it look as though the company is purposefully saving income for a later year?
Accrued and deferred expenses	• Are there significant accrued expenses relative to net income, and do they fluctuate by large amounts? • Are there any deferred expenses listed as assets on the balance sheet (other than deferred taxes)? • Are there any unusual assets or unexplained large increases in assets, particularly relative to the increase in revenues?
Deferred taxes	• Does the company's net deferred tax impact on net income fluctuate from a positive to a negative impact? • Does the company have significant deferred tax assets? Is it plausible that they will be usable in subsequent years? • Did the company establish a valuation allowance for deferred tax assets, and has it fluctuated in value over time?
Contingencies and reserves	• Scrutinize disclosures both on the balance sheet and footnotes for: • Contingent losses. • Contingent liabilities. • Reserves. • Derivative liabilities. • Similar terminology. • Consider whether the company appears to be creating a cookie jar reserve.

Overstated Operating Cash Flow

Acceleration of cash received for revenues or deferral of cash paid for expenses	• Look for factoring, sales of receivables, or other transactions to bring cash flow in early. • See if the company is delaying payments to suppliers and others, such as an increase in accounts payable.
Borrowing transactions treated as operating cash inflow	• Are there contingent or other off-balance sheet liabilities disclosed (or not disclosed)? • Look for reciprocal or repurchase agreements/insurance type contracts. • Is there any revenue from an unusual type customer (financial services firm)?

(Continued)

EXHIBIT 7.2 *Continued*

Expenditures improperly classified as capital expenditures	• Are there abnormal increases in long-term assets? • Are there unusual assets? • Any abnormal changes in capital expenditures?

Evaluating Governance, Auditor, and Related-Party Issues

Board governance and independence	• Examine board membership for external members. Corporate governance is weak for boards comprised of less than 50% independent nonexecutive directors. • Be wary when the CEO also serves as chairman of the board of directors. • Are there separate board audit, nomination, and compensation committees composed primarily of independent directors? If not, exercise more due diligence. • Examine possible interlocking directors.
Shareowner rights	• Are there different classes of shares, and how do voting rights differ between them? If so, are there safeguards in the articles of organization or bylaws that protect the rights and interests of those shareowners whose shares have inferior rights? • Was the company recently privatized by a government or government entity with retained voting rights that could veto certain decisions of management and the board? • Are shareholders able to vote their shares by proxy if they are unable to attend a shareowners' meeting, cast confidential votes, submit matters to a vote, and approve changes to corporate structure and policies?
Interlocking ownership or directorships	• Are there interlocking ownership or directorship arrangements? If so, increase analysis and due diligence.
Related-party issues	• Are there business transactions between company and management? • Are family members of management involved in the company or other companies that the subject company does business with? • Are there significant loans to management or affiliated companies from either the company or related entities?
Excessive compensation and personal use of assets	• Are there sufficient and clear disclosures of compensation or perks of management so that they can be evaluated with reference to similar companies? • Are there sufficient internal controls to prevent personal use or expropriation of corporate assets? • Is there excessive use of stock-based compensation/options?
Lack of transparency	• Does the company resist making detailed disclosures or use language that obscures what is going on?

EXHIBIT 7.2 *Continued*

Auditor issues	• Are auditors truly independent and objective? Are there any conditions that may impair their objectivity? Is the audit firm large enough, and does it have a quality reputation to audit a public company? • Have there been resignations of, frequent changes in, or disagreements with auditors? • Is there a strong independent audit committee of the board and strong internal control to mitigate other issues?

in Exhibit 7.2, and highlight anything that appears on this checklist such as unusual assets, accounting policies, related-party transactions, and auditor changes, just to name a few. Also, watch for any changes between the sets of financial statements over time and for any items on this list or any amendments made to prior-year financial statements in any set of statements. Compare accounting policies to those of peers to determine whether the subject company is being aggressive. Look for items disclosed in the footnotes but not reflected on the financial statements (losses or off-balance-sheet financing). Assess the strength of corporate governance by examining information on the board, management, and auditors.

- *Prepare a common-size analysis of the income statement.* This is done by dividing all items on the income statement in each year by revenue for each year. Examine any major changes in these percentages over time. Compare the company's expenses and subtotals as a percentage of revenue (gross margin, operating margin, profit margin) to peer companies, and ascertain the reasons for any differences. Look for any unusual income or gain items listed in the operating section or unusual losses or expenses listed in the non-operating section.
- *Prepare a common-size analysis of the balance sheet.* This is done by dividing all items on the balance sheet for each year by total assets for that year. Examine major changes in these percentages over time. Look for unusual assets or large increases in assets. Compare the company's common-size balance sheet percentages to peer companies, and ascertain whether there are any items that are significantly different. Examine the owners' equity portion of the balance sheet in particular to determine if any losses bypassed the income statement and retained earnings.
- *Analyze the cash flow statement.* Place the income statement and cash flow statement for all years side by side and look for discrepancies between them (e.g., increasing earnings but decreasing operating cash flows). Examine all reconciling items between net income and operating cash flow in the operating section of the cash flow statement. Make sure you understand large items, and look for any significant trends or changes over time. Ideally, you would like to see operating cash flow higher than net income in the aggregate over all periods—if it is not, then dig a little deeper to understand why.

- *Do a ratio analysis of the financial statements.* Examine the trend in the company's ratios over time and relative to peer companies with a particular focus on:
  - Receivables turnover or days' receivable (indicating whether receivables are growing faster than revenues).
  - Inventory turnover or days' inventory (indicating whether there might be a buildup or overstatement of inventory).
  - Total asset turnover and return on assets (with a particular focus on whether the company's balance sheet supports its operations).
- *Seek out independent information on the company.* If the company must file other types of reports (e.g., local sales tax returns) with other entities, such as governmental or regulatory agencies, compare those reports to the information in the financial statements. Compare information on asset ownership (e.g., real estate records) where available to assets listed on the balance sheet. Examine any financial statements of other entities the company does business with or other companies where management or the directors have an interest. Look for independent data on revenues, including personal visits and observations if possible.

PARTING COMMENTS

Unscrupulous companies will continue to innovate at the types of accounting games that they play (recall Sino-Forest techniques to offset receivables increases). Fortunately, most accounting games today are still relatively similar to those from decades ago. Ultimately, there are limited ways to cook the books, and the accounting frameworks presented here should help you detect accounting fraud in spite of its continuing evolution. The level and depth of analysis needed to detect potential accounting games is high but can be well worth the effort if it can prevent you from making a costly investment mistake. It may also enable you to identify opportunities to take a short position in securities.

CASE STUDIES

The following cases examine companies that may have been accused—but not necessarily ascertained guilty—of manipulating their reported results. These cases demonstrate many of the concepts presented in this chapter. Note that some concepts in these cases may be related to concepts covered in other chapters; however the full case is included for completeness and to demonstrate that there is often a plural nature of accounting manipulation.

Case 7.1: Celltrion, Inc.

Background

- Celltrion, Inc. is a biopharmaceutical company, involved in the development and manufacture of biosimilar products, which are less expensive versions of complex biological drugs used to treat diseases such as cancer, utilizing DNA technology and cell culture techniques. Celltrion, headquartered in Incheon, is South Korea's biggest manufacturer of antibody biosimilars and the largest company on the junior KOSDAQ bourse, with a market capitalization of 4.8 trillion won in early 2013 (US$4.4 billion).
- The company's CEO and founder, Seo Jung-Jin, announced in May 2013 that he was tired of "having to fight this costly battle with speculative short-sellers" and was putting his interest in the company (roughly 25 percent) on the block.
- Temasek Holdings Pte. Ltd. is the second-largest shareholder of Celltrion, and has an option to sell its 10.5 percent stake in Celltrion if Seo decides to continue with the sale of his stake, potentially increasing the size of the sale to $1.7 billion from $1.4 billion.
- Potential bidders of the stake in Celltrion have been dissuaded on the back of rumors regarding accounting fraud and clinical trial failures.

What Happened

- The Financial Supervisory Service (FSS) in Korea launched a formal investigation into the allegations in April 2013. Celltrion shares dipped after Korea's Yonhap news agency and broadcaster SBS CNBC reported the insider trading allegations. The Capital Market Investigation and Review Committee of the FSS has not provided any updates of its findings on Celltrion to date.
- Regarding the deterioration of its stock price, Celltrion has released a statement that it was "dumbfounded" by the circulation of unconfirmed new reports, with the firm turning around and requesting the FSS to investigate short-sellers that it claims have been trying to manipulate its stock price.
- FSS said in a statement, "It was Seo who manipulated the stock price. He inflated Celltrion's stock price because some of its affiliates, including Celltrion GSC, had received loans from Banks backed by their stake in the bio firm." They reasoned that "the affiliates had to pay back loans or provide more collateral should Celltrion's stock price fall. That's why Seo attempted to keep its stock price high."

Warning Signs

- Allegations of accounting fraud within Celltrion revolved around the related-party transactions with its unlisted affiliate, Celltrion Healthcare. They stem from the fact that sales of Celltrion are made up largely of sales to Celltrion Healthcare, where inventory has been increasing as the company awaits regulatory approvals in Europe. In the most recent six-month-period filing, 98.2 percent of total sales, 140 billion won, were to Celltrion Healthcare. Celltrion Healthcare's inventory balance also increased by nearly 300 billion won last year to 679 billion won.

- In his defense, Seo claimed that "(Celltrion) Healthcare has only nine months of inventory, which is the lowest level for the industry. They need inventory build-up to ensure smooth supply as soon as regulatory approval is received."
- A potential red flag for investors is when they notice management of the company selling off a large portion of their holdings. This would indicate a misalignment of interest between the management and shareholders. Over the span of four days at the start of April, one of the co-presidents at Celltrion, Hong Seung Seo, divested roughly 50 percent of his holdings in Celltrion, or 57,500 shares. This move came just over a week before the stock price of Celltrion dived on the back of insider trading allegations.

Key Lessons

- *Alignment of interests.* Once again we have a case where the priorities/interests of the management do not lie with the shareholders of the company. Similar to the case regarding PUDA and SinoEnv, when the management actively divested its holdings in the company, such incidents amplify the possibility that management might choose to act in their own interest rather than in the best interest of the shareholders. In this case, we have Seo, the company's founder, publicly announcing his plans to sell off his entire stake in the company. More worrying still is Celltrion's co-president selling 50 percent of his holdings into the open market, just two weeks before the share price took a huge hit.
- *Related-party transactions.* There is (can be?) a tendency for business owners to build an intricate web of subsidiaries and affiliates, often for legitimate reasons such as the separation of business units and geographical diversification. However, every so often, some of these webs are set out to mislead and disguise the basis of transactions from the curious analysts. The percentage of sales that Celltrion Healthcare accounts for on the books of Celltrion, Inc. should set off an instant red flag and prompt any responsible analyst to investigate further.

Case 7.2: Real Gold Mining

Background

- Real Gold Mining is an investment holding company engaged in the exploration, mining, and processing of gold ore and sale of concentrates in Inner Mongolia, China. The company's principal product is gold concentrate—the raw material used in gold smelting operations to produce standard and nonstandard gold.

- The company is registered in the Cayman Islands and, through its subsidiaries, has three 97.1–percent–owned mining properties in Chifeng.
- The company's sources of revenue are the three gold mines located in the Chifeng Municipality in Inner Mongolia: Nantaizi, Shirengou, and Luotuochang.
- Real Gold was listed on the Hong Kong Exchange (HKEX) in February 2009, raising approximately HKD 1 billion at HKD 6.25 per share. The underwriters were Citi and Macquarie.
- In June 2010, Real Gold Mining raised a further HKD 1.2 billion at HKD 12.15 per share. Citi was the broker.
- Before trading in the company was halted in May 2011, it was valued at HKD 8.1 billion on the HKEX, with 908.8 million shares outstanding and a free float of 429.4 million shares.
- Real Gold's subsidiaries included Lita Investment Ltd., Rich Vision Holdings Ltd., Fubon Industrial (Huizhou) Co. Ltd., and Chifeng Fuqiao Mining Co. Ltd.
- In April 2010, the company acquired Jinshi Mining, and in June 2010 acquired Great Future Investments Ltd. and Yuanyi Mining.
- Revenue from mining of gold was the main source of overall profit for Real Gold, accounting for 89 percent in 2007, 71 percent in 2008, 66.1 percent in 2009, and 64.1 percent in 2010.
- In the company's annual report for 2008, 2009, and 2010, the gross profit margin and cost of sales percentages were constant. This was in spite of gold prices fluctuating from a low of US$690/oz. to a high of US$1,420/oz. between 2008 and 2010.

  Annual Report 2008 – The Company recorded revenue of approximately RMB312.3M, representing an increase of 3,800 percent over 2007. Gross profit was RMB231.7M, with gross margin of 74.2 percent and cost of sales about 25.8 percent of revenue.

  Annual Report 2009: Gross profit margin was 74.1 percent, and cost of sales was 25.9 percent.

  Annual Report 2010: Gross profit margin was 77.3 percent, and cost of sales was 22.7 percent.

  Cost of sales constituted the cost of raw materials consumed, subcontracting fees, auxiliary material costs, electricity costs, depreciation/amortization, environmental protection fees, and production safety fees.
- Real Gold Mining's auditor: Deloitte.
- Major shareholders of the company:
  - Lead Honest Management: 52.8 percent
  - Citigroup Inc.: 27 percent
  - Value Partners: 8.6 percent
  - Deutsche Bank: 4.9 percent

    Lead Honest Management is a British Virgin Islands (BVI)-based vehicle and is 100 percent controlled by Tercel Holdings Ltd., which in turn is controlled by Credit Suisse Trust Ltd. Credit Suisse Trust Ltd. is a trustee of Tercel Trust.

Ruilin Wu is the founder of Tercel Trust. The beneficiaries of Tercel Trust include Wu's family members.

- Lu Tianjun (chairman), Ma Wenxue (head of Ore Processing), and Cui Jie (CFO) are directors of Chifeng Fuqiao Mining Co., an investment company that is 97.1 percent owned by Real Gold. All three sit on the board of directors.

Chifeng Fuqiao owns Yuanyi Mining and Jinshi Mining—two mines under the People's Republic of China (PRC) reporting standards (not the Joint Ore Reserves Committee), with small quantities of gold ore.

What Happened

- In May 2011, the *South China Morning Post* (SCMP) reported that Real Gold's FY2009 accounts filed with the HKEX did not match the accounts lodged with China's State Administration of Industry & Commerce (SAIC).
- In response, Real Gold stated that the data company Qingdao Inter-Credit provided SCMP with incorrect figures. Qingdao Inter-Credit insisted its figures were accurate.
- On 27 May 2011, Real Gold's shares were suspended when the HKEX stepped in to investigate.
- It was later revealed that Ruilin Wu had covertly pledged all of Real Gold's assets to secure personal loans from Shanghai Pudong Development Bank (SPD).
- According to documents obtained from the Huizhou Administration of Industry and Commerce (HAIC) in October 2010, Wu arranged a RMB$240 million (HKD 288 million) borrowing facility with SPD for four private companies that are part of his Cosun telecommunications-to-mining conglomerate. Wu also signed a similar pledge with SPD for a RMB$100 million borrowing facility in September 2009.
- In both instances, Wu pledged the entire issued share capital of Real Gold's unit Fubon Industrial Huizhou Co. as security to SPD for loans for non–Real Gold entities. Fubon Industrial owns all of Real Gold's three mines.
- On 16 June 2011, Real Gold announced that Wu, the controlling shareholder, had resigned as a director due to inappropriately pledging Real Gold's shares to obtain personal loans. Wu resigned from Real Gold's subsidiary, Lita Investments, and no longer held any position in Real Gold.
- Real Gold has insisted that none of its board of directors, led by current chairman Lu Tianjun, were aware of Wu's asset pledges until contacted by SCMP on 13 June.
- On 20 June 2011, Real Gold announced it was released from the loan pledges made improperly by Wu.
- In August 2011, news of the Securities and Financial Commission (SFC) investigation came on the heels of an announcement from Real Gold that

approximately HKD 1.5 billion of company funds had been secretly funneled to majority shareholder Wu Ruilin. Real Gold had also lent Wu HKD 955 million, of which HKD 316 million was still outstanding on 30 June 2011, according to an exchange filing of 22 August.

- In addition, Real Gold admitted that, in the first half of 2011, the company purchased two phosphorous mines in Mongolia from Wu for an additional HKD 520 million, without disclosing the connected transaction or obtaining shareholder approval.
- In August 2011, independent director Wan Kam To, who was leading an internal investigation of the allegations, resigned after disagreeing with the board on the approach and timing of the probe.
- In October 2011, auditor Deloitte announced that its report on Real Gold's FY2010 earnings was not reliable because Real Gold failed to disclose material information. Deloitte also announced its resignation as auditor.
- In 2013, Real Gold was suspended from trading for another two years.

Warning Signs

- Wang Zhentian, chairman at time of the initial public offering, resigned in May 2009.
- CEO Qiu Haicheng resigned in May 2011 and was replaced by an internal candidate, vice chairman Ma Wenxue.
- Ruilin Wu, a telecoms-to-mining magnate who was the founder of Real Gold, was not on Real Gold's main board. He was instead a director on one of its subsidiaries, Lita Investments. This was stated in the initial public offering (IPO) prospectus and annual reports. In addition, Wu was recorded as also having a short position on Real Gold covering 25.8 percent.
- In the 2010 annual report, the "loans payable" footnote stated that the company had entered into two sets of loan arrangements with two separate independent third parties and their respective affiliates in China.

    Real Gold advanced HKD 415.1 million and US$9 million and upon receipt of the funds by the two parties, the affiliates advanced funds of an equivalent amount in RMB427.4 million to a Chinese subsidiary of Real Gold. There was no legally enforceable right of Real Gold to set off the loans receivable and loans payable. Further research into the identities of the two independent third parties did not turn up any names.

Key Lessons

- *Statements from independent technical reports, even from global consultancies— BEHRE DOLBEAR Asia (BDASIA)—should not be taken wholesale.* Real Gold's IPO prospectus showed BDASIA rating Real Gold's risk analysis as moderate risk only in "mining" and "production targets." The rest of the risk components of the three mines saw low and low-to-moderate risks.

The BDASIA team consisted of senior-level mining professionals from the Denver office in the United States, Sydney, and London, where they visited the sites in October 2007. Real Gold was listed in February 2009.

What was not stated in the prospectus was where BDASIA got the data. BDASIA did not undertake an audit of Real Gold's data, re-estimate mineral resources, nor review tenement status with respect to legal or statutory issues. This was stated in Appendix V, V-2 of the IPO prospectus.

The technical report that BDASIA stated in the IPO prospectus was not the original version from the Liaoning Geological Exploration Institute, which calculated the mining assets for the three gold mines in July 2007. Liaoning Geological has links to the Ministry of Land and Resources of the PRC.

Investigative research from *China Economic Times* stated that Real Gold hired two companies to do geological reports for the same mines, with the intention of increasing reserves by substituting real data with fake data. The reports would be revised to create fake information, though layman investors would not be able to detect the fraud because of the technicalities.

After the Liaoning Geological Exploration Institute was finished, Chifeng Shengyuan Geological Exploration Limited produced another three detailed exploration reports for Real Gold. These were then given to BDASIA, which the consultancy put into the IPO prospectus as stating low to moderate risk.

Insiders told *China Economic Times* that it is well known that mining consultancies such as BDASIA are usually not allowed to go to the real mine sites they are hired to do reporting on. Mining companies would take them to other mining sites instead. In order to get the real original report, one would need to go to the Record Office in Inner Mongolia's Department of Land and Resources.

- *If there is no mine safety license, production is not to be regarded as legal production.* Inner Mongolia's Bureau of Land and Resources was making huge efforts to renew the Luotuochang mine's related licenses, despite the mines being closed and the mining license having been expired for five months. The Bureau of Land and Resources allowed Real Gold to renew the mining license despite the Luotuochang mine's not being in operation because Real Gold paid for the mineral resource compensation fee, which amounted to RMB$242,000. This allowed the company to report to the Bureau that the mine's deposits would allow for a higher level of production than was actually possible. As the supervisory departments were getting paid, none of the departments were willing to investigate Real Gold.

- *Phantom customers.* The IPO prospectus stated Real Gold's five major clients: Liaoning Xindu Gold Ltd. Co., Henan Yuguang Gold & Lead Ltd., Chifeng Kumbahongye Zinc Ltd. Co., Chifeng Baiyinnuo'er Lead & Zinc Factory, and Chifeng Fubang Copper Ltd. No specific sales volume for each client was revealed in the annual reports.

China Economic Times reported that three of the clients had no business relationship existing with Real Gold. Only Chifeng Fubang Copper Ltd. confirmed that it was a customer.

Case 7.3: Fibrechem Technologies Ltd.

Background

- Fibrechem Technologies is a Bermudan registered company listed on the Singapore Exchange (SGX) with a market capitalization of S$95 million. It owns Hong Kong and Chinese subsidiaries that manufacture polyester fibers and microfiber leather at three manufacturing plants in Fujian Province, China. The founder, James Zhang, and his family control 32 percent of the equity.
- Business performance:
  - In the 12 months ending September 2008, reported revenues of HKD 1.98 billion (up from HKD 300 million in FY2003); earnings before interest, taxes, depreciation, and amortization (EBITDA) of HKD 728 million; and net profit after tax of HKD 546 million. The company appeared to be rapidly growing and profitable. It paid dividends of HKD 82 million (HKD 0.09 per share) in 2008, a payout ratio of 15 percent.
- Capital structure (at end of September 2008):
  - Cash of HKD 1.2 billion (US$150 million), representing 32 percent of total assets (up from US$15 million in June 2006).
  - Net working capital of HKD 296.7 million (US$38.3 million).
    - Receivables of HKD 280 million (US$36.1 million) (up from US$12 million in June 2006).
    - Inventories of HKD 94.6 million (US$12.2 million).
    - Payables of HKD 78 million (US$10 million).
  - Bank loans of HKD 622 million.

What Happened

- On 25 February 2009, the company announced the following:
  - Its auditors (Deloitte & Touche) would not sign off on its 2008 fiscal year audit following difficulties determining cash and account receivables.
  - James Zhang resigned as executive chairman and CEO.
  - Company appointed local insolvency expert Ntan Advisory as an independent investigator and financial adviser.
- Fibrechem's shares have remained in suspension since the announcement.
  - In December 2011, Ntan released its investigative report, which took three years to complete.
  - The report uncovered financial and accounting irregularities and concluded that the fraud was probably carried out at the direction or with the knowledge of the PRC management, in particular the chairman/CEO and CFO.
  - Key findings include:
    - Overstatement of assets by HKD 382 million (US$49 million) and cash balance by HKD 686 million (US$88 million).
    - Unaccounted cash balance of HKD 777 million (US$100 million), which may have been embezzled.

- Improper and incomplete disclosure of assets and liabilities, including defaulted loans from Chinese banks.
- Unapproved transfer of controlling stake in key operating company to a subsidiary that is out of reach of offshore creditors.
- Crucially, Ntan's investigations were hindered by the lack of statutory coercive powers to force cooperation by employees and relevant parties in China, resulting in limited access to subsidiary accounting records and missing or unreliable accounts.
- Representatives from PricewaterhouseCoopers have been provisionally appointed to liquidate the company.

Warning Signs

- Excessive cash reserves in relation to the company's size and its capital expenditure (capex) plans:
  - Company raised US$107 million of preferred equity and debt in 2007/2008 to fund the expansion, but then covered capex from operating cash flows during 2008.
  - Not much cash ever returned to shareholders through cash dividends, sub–15 percent cash payout ratio since listing.
  - Company then raised senior loans to fund capex, subordinating the earlier capital providers.
- Cash reserves were held offshore/limited disclosure:
  - Only 1 percent of the company's deposits were held in the listed company, and it did not disclose which entities in the group held the remaining cash.
  - Agriculture Bank of China is the only bank listed as a principal banker.
  - Can offshore auditors (even the "Big 4") really verify Chinese deposits to international standards?
- Company was increasing long-term borrowings despite holding large cash reserves.
  - Cash reserves actually increased US$13 million in the first nine months of 2008 as the company drew an additional US$30 million of debt.
  - Company explained its offshore borrowings as a natural hedge as it was borrowing in U.S. dollars and its major products are priced in U.S. dollars.
- Poor working capital management/limited disclosures:
  - Increasing working capital cash cycle without adequate explanation.
  - Company's stated policy is to make provisions for irrecoverable receivables greater than 60 days. No provisions were made in fiscal year 2007 or 2008.
- Complicated organization structure:
  - Capital injected from listed company as equity onshore into China or as unsecured nonguaranteed loans to offshore entities, then sent on as equity.
  - Listing company has no creditor claims against any of the operating companies or assets.

- Fibrechem's earnings before interest and taxes (EBIT) margins were double its larger competitors and very stable for a cyclical industry.
  - If its niche were truly that profitable and growing rapidly, where was the new competition?
- Founder issues:
  - The major shareholder was known to have pledged his shares to fund other business ventures in China.
  - The chairman and his family are known to have multiple business ventures in Fujian province, China; listed as one of the top 1,000 richest businessmen in China.
  - Founder/Chairman had changed his citizenship from China to Dominican Republic.
- Complicated organizational structure never gave a clear picture in public accounts how its Chinese subsidiaries were capitalized.
- Inter-company sales doubled to 13.1 percent of sales in FY2007.
- Questionable internal audit and accounting standards:
  - It is unclear how much access to the operating subsidiaries accounts was requested by the company's audit committee composed of the independent Singapore-based directors.
  - Company had no executive internal auditor; all testing of internal controls was conducted by an external professional services firm.
  - Audit Committee had access to an external accounting firm to report on internal compliance systems, but this was not the external auditor, Deloitte & Touche.

Key Lessons

- It is difficult for investors and boards of foreign-listed Chinese companies to monitor and control onshore operating subsidiaries.
- Poor corporate governance and a complicated organizational structure can enable accounting games to be played.
- Be wary of excess cash reserves, particularly when the company continues to borrow. This is an indicator that they need cash and the reported cash balances may not exist.

REFERENCES

Fibrecham Technologies. 2011. Limited Report of the Independent Investigation by Ntan Corporate Advisory Pte. Ltd., December 1.

Na Jeong-ju. 2013. "Celltrion CEO Under Scrutiny," *Korea Times*, September 16.

Real Gold IPO Prospectus. February 10, 2009.

Real Gold Mining Annual Reports for 2008, 2009 and 2010.
South China Morning Post articles regarding Real Gold Mining:
   "Accounting Mystery for Mining Firm," May 27, 2011.
   "Real Gold Halts Trading after Filing Questioned," May 28, 2011.
   "Real Gold's Wu Resigns Over Loan Pledges," June 21, 2011.
   "SFC Probing Real Gold Mining," August 24, 2011.

ABOUT THE AUTHORS

ChinHwee Tan, CFA, CPA, is the founding partner in Asia for a leading global alternative investor, among the top largest in the world. He was voted by the *Hedge Fund Journal* as one of the emerging top 40 absolute return investors globally, and was also named Best Asia Credit Hedge Fund Manager by *The Asset*. Mr. Tan has been honored as a World Economic Forum Young Global Leader and is the winner of the 2013 Distinguished Financial Industry Certified Professional (FICP) Award from the Singapore government. He is a member of the Resource Panel for Government Parliamentary Committee for Finance and Trade and Industry for the Singapore government and sits on the panel on Private Equity for the Monetary Authority of Singapore. Mr. Tan is active in serving the community and sits on various for-profit and not-for-profit boards. Mr. Tan is an adjunct professor in a number of universities teaching forensic accounting. He enjoys spending time with his three young children.

Thomas R. Robinson, CFA, CPA, is managing director of the Americas at CFA Institute, leading a cross-functional team that participates in developing global strategy, implements the global strategy regionally, and engages with stakeholders regionally. Previously, Mr. Robinson served as managing director of education at CFA Institute providing vision and leadership for a 100-member global team producing and delivering educational content for candidates, members, and other investment professionals Prior to joining the CFA Institute, he had a 25-year career in financial services and education, having served as a tenured faculty member at the University of Miami, managing director of a private wealth investment advisory firm, and director of tax and consulting services at a public accounting firm. Mr. Robinson has published regularly in academic and professional journals and has authored or coauthored many books on financial analysis valuation and wealth management. He is a CFA charterholder, a Certified Public Accountant (CPA) (Ohio), a Certified Financial Planner (CFP®), and a Chartered Alternative Investment Analyst (CAIA). He holds a bachelor's degree in economics from the University of Pennsylvania, and a master's and doctorate from Case Western Reserve University.

INDEX

Printed and bound by CPI Group (UK) Ltd, Croydon, CR0 4YY

21/04/2025

14659497-0002